Travels wit

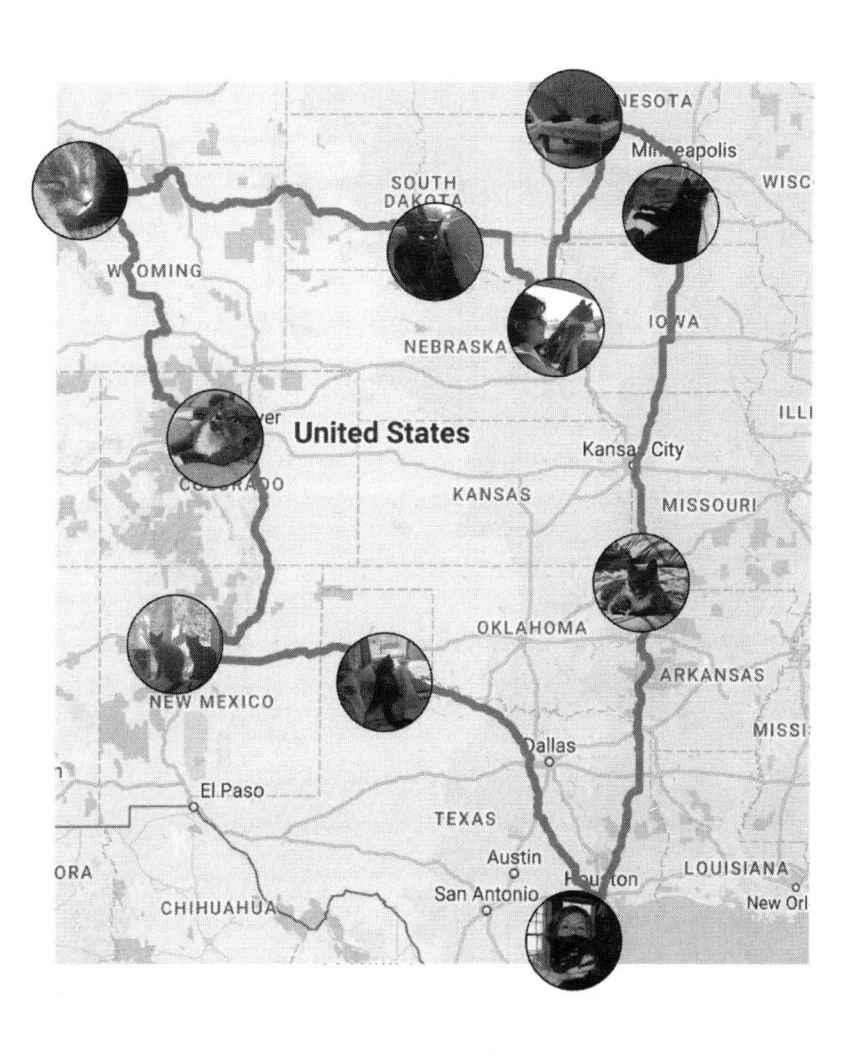

Travels with Cats

by Anne Leonard

Copyright © 2018. All Rights Reserved

Edited by Cheryl Lim

Cover design and formatting by Bernadette Payne

Photos by Anne Leonard and Mike Badger

Without limiting the rights under copyright reserved above, no part of this publication may be reproduced, stored, or introduced into a retrieval system, or transmitted in any form, or by any means (electronically, mechanical, photocopying, recording or otherwise) without the proper written permission of the copyright owner, except in the case of brief quotations embodied in critical articles and reviews.

Dedication

To all my lost loves, both human and feline.

And to Sauks and Andy, my reluctant companions on the road.

—Anne

'Tis better to have loved and lost

Than never to have loved at all.

—Alfred, Lord Tennyson

Time present and time past
Are both perhaps present in time future
And time future contained in time past.
If all time is eternally present
All time is unredeemable.

….

In my end is my beginning.

—T. S. Eliot, The Four Quartets

Table of Contents

Part 1: Broken Circles 9

    Chapter 1: Losing Husbands and Cats 10

    Chapter 2: Leaving Sugar Land 25

    Chapter 3: My first day in the west 34

    Chapter 4: Crossing the state line 39

Part 2: Tijeras, New Mexico, June 5-July 31 47

    Chapter 5: Staking Out Our New Territory 48

    Chapter 6: From Flood to Fire 54

    Chapter 7: All cats stay indoors 61

    Chapter 8: Black Cat Art 67

    Chapter 9: Service Animals 75

    Chapter 10: Seeing the light 84

Part 3: Leaving the West 91

    Chapter 11: The adventure begins 92

    Chapter 12: Princess Fifi (April 29, 2005-August 1, 2016) 99

    Chapter 13: Sauks's faux paw 110

    Chapter 14: A drug deal 116

    Chapter 15: Sauks discovers automatic windows 123

    Chapter 16: Scary neighbors 131

Chapter 17: Dead Indians 143

Chapter 18: Heading east 150

Part 4: The long road home.. 157

Chapter 19: God's Country and Grandma's 158

Chapter 20: There's no place like Wayne................................ 163

Chapter 21: A basement birthday celebration........................ 171

Chapter 22: Other people's plans 178

Chapter 23: I still don't make it to North Dakota................... 183

Chapter 24: Cabin fever.. 191

Chapter 25: Hotel hell.. 204

Chapter 26: Still singing the blues 208

Chapter 27: Back to civilization 214

Chapter 28: Minnesota living 218

Chapter 29: One long-ass day.. 226

Chapter 30: Almost home.. 231

Epilogue... 239

v

Prologue

"You are discriminating against a perfectly nice cat."

I was in Northfield, Minnesota, and this proclamation was the low point of my summer on the road with cats. At the time, I knew I was making an ass of myself, and my behavior is still cringe-worthy upon reflection. But it was 6:30 in the evening and I had two weary cats baking in a car on the sunny side of Division Street.

My outburst followed a good twenty minutes of pleading my case with a sullen hotel desk clerk who'd made it clear even before the cat issue came up that she had better things to do than deal with the likes of me. We had reached an impasse and I had to concede that the historic Archer House was not going to make an exception to their rule that their pet rooms are reserved for dogs but definitely not cats.

What made it even worse was I had only myself to blame for blurting out I had a cat (never mind it was actually two). My credit card had been run and I had the old-fashioned room key in hand. If I hadn't opened my big mouth the desk clerk, every bit as unfriendly as the one who'd taken my reservation on the phone the previous evening, would have no doubt quickly retreated to her computer some distance behind the expansive mahogany reception desk.

That's where she'd been parked when I'd arrived, reluctantly rising with a heavy sigh and a frown at my appearance. I guessed she was a bored college student, a distinct possibility since

Northfield is home to not one but two posh institutes of higher learning. And considering she was the very antithesis of Minnesota nice, probably an out-of-state student at that. Once back at her station—no doubt perusing Facebook—she probably wouldn't have noticed if I'd traipsed through the elegant antique-filled lobby with an elephant.

Seasoned traveler that I am, I had carefully studied the Archer House website prior to booking. In addition to claiming to be pet friendly, it said they had off-street parking that accessed an elevator. I'd noticed that elevator upon entry. It was conveniently located around the corner from the front desk. Perfect. No hauling first one cat, then another, and then a litter box, up the red-carpeted grand staircase. Rather, we'd go straight up to our second-floor room, albeit it in three, if not four trips.

"Park on the street," the desk clerk had said.

"But your website said not to."

"This time of day it doesn't matter."

"How about in the morning?"

"Before eleven no one cares." Apparently, it took more energy than she was willing to explain how one accessed their parking lot.

That was when I made my big mistake. "I do have a pet room, right? I requested one when I booked last night."

I'd finally piqued her interest.

"What kind of pet?" she asked suspiciously.

The rest is history. I stormed out, loudly tossing my discrimination charge over my shoulder. The two guests who had been patiently waiting to check in behind me quickly looked away, no doubt fearing to make eye contact with the mad woman bolting toward the door who obviously was not a Minnesotan. I stomped down the wide veranda and got in my car. The cats, whom had been anticipating a change in scenery, slunk back into their riding positions.

I was back out on the highway before I calmed down enough to pull over and find the number for the AmericInn. In the three weeks since I'd left New Mexico I'd found this Minnesota-based chain to be clean, comfortable, and reliably pet friendly. It had been my first choice until I'd spotted the words "accepts pets" during a random perusal of the Archer House website. It had seemed odd for a nineteenth century four-story red brick hotel with dormer windows and block-long front porch. Frosted with fancy white woodwork and crowned with a mansard roof, the historic hotel is a renowned setting for weddings and other celebrations rather than a respite for road warriors with pets in tow. That was precisely the reason that rather than book online with a few clicks, I'd called the night to confirm they indeed took pets and request a pet room. That said, the desk clerk who'd taken my reservation sounded sleepy and bored and had left me with a nagging sense of unease. Knowing I should have just heeded my intuition now fueled my anger.

After a series of deep breaths, I called the AmericInn and with as much calm as I could muster asked if they had a room. They did and confirmed they take cats. Or cat in the singular, as once again I didn't mention I had two, which is a sure sign of lunacy. It proved to be a wise move as when I signed their pet policy I noted they only allow one animal per room.

"Cats are easier than dogs," my friend Susie had said when I'd visited her two weeks earlier. She was referring to low-maintenance feline traits like using a litter box and ability to survive for days without human assistance.

Yes, if you leave them at home. On the road, not so much.

So how was it that I spent the summer of 2016 traveling more than 4,700 miles through eleven states with two cats? My journey began the Friday after Memorial Day when I left my home in the Houston suburb of Sugar Land to spend two months in the Sandia Mountains just east of Albuquerque. Then, like a cat chasing its tail, I slowly made my way back to Texas during August by circling the mid-section of the country. Northfield was the latest in a series of stops that included Denver and Vail in Colorado; Cody, Wyoming; Chamberlain, South Dakota; Wayne, Nebraska; and Alexandria, Minnesota.

Quite frankly I neither recommend nor hope to repeat such a trip, even though Sauks and Andy were exceptional travelers – albeit on the low bar of feline tolerance for transportation. But 2016 was yet another year of loss, and loss for me always brings on a bad case of wanderlust.

A friend recently noted that when a man's world falls apart, say in a divorce, his impulse is to hunker down. A woman's, at least in our modern age, seems to be to find answers in far-flung experiences and encounters. Such has been the case with me, with 2016 being an example as my world once again fell apart when I was unexpectedly laid off early in the year. The last time I had been without employment was thirty-five years earlier.

I was used to losing husbands and cats, not jobs. In a span of twelve years and two months, I was widowed twice. My first husband Don died in January 1997, followed by my second husband Mike in March 2009. Eerily, I lost a black cat just days before each husband's death, Arthur and Sammy, respectively. And it didn't stop there. While Mike and I were together, I lost Murphy, my much-loved tabby who'd provided so much comfort during Don's illness. And after Mike died, I lost another two cats to devastating illnesses, Jack two months to the day after Mike, and Fig several years later.

So, I had had more than my share of loss in the past two decades, losing husbands Don and Mike, and cats Arthur, Murphy, Sam, Jack, and Fig. Or, in chronological order without the sorting between humans and felines: Arthur, Don, Murphy, Sam, Mike, Jack, and Fig. If you've had a hard time keeping up, don't worry: I provide a handy chart in Chapter 1.

On the heels of all that pain, losing my job was a larger shock than I could have imagined. After more than three decades of working in the oil industry, my luck with good-old-boy politics and bosses who have little tolerance for ornery, outspoken women finally ran out. I'd become complacent over the years, so was oblivious to the warning signs of inciting two bosses at two different companies into a frothing-at-the-mouth rage within three short years. On the first Wednesday of February 2016, I was ignominiously sent packing. It was a dirty deal and a boring story, so I'll weave in a few details here and there and omit the rest.

Losing my job dealt a major blow to my ego. Through all the turmoil I'd endured, my job was a constant. I was an oil and gas editor, one of just a few women amongst a legion of men. I worked hard, was well paid, good at what I did, and the beneficiary of world travel. Now all of that was gone.

So, who am I now? Well, during the summer of 2016 as I traveled the American West my name—channeling Kevin Costner's Academy winning role—could have been Travels with Cats. Aptly enough, the cats and I stumbled across a film set for *Dancing with Wolves* during our summer travels.

By the way, if I have somehow enticed anyone to stay at the Archer House, note that their surly service is somewhat offset by the excellence of the on-site Indian restaurant. It was one of the reasons I'd ventured to Northfield in the first place, and such is my love of Indian food that after settling the cats into yet-another AmericInn overlooking grain elevators (just like the one I'd stayed at in South Dakota) I returned to the scene of the crime. I had hoped to enter Chapati Cuisine of India from the street, but alas the only entrance was through the hotel lobby. This gave me pause, but I put my head down and plowed ahead, not daring to look toward the front desk.

The lamb vindaloo was well worth the walk of shame.

Part 1: Broken Circles

Chapter 1: Losing Husbands and Cats

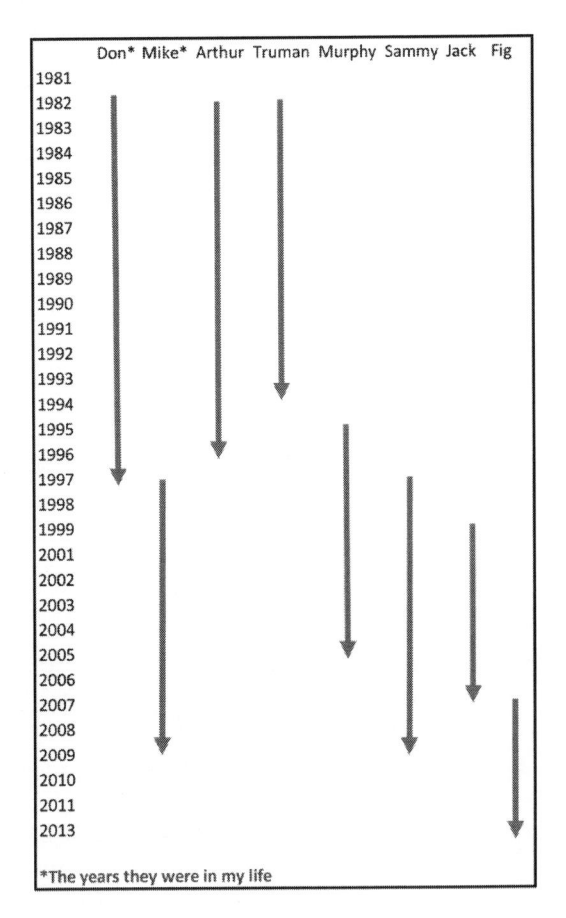

	Don*	Mike*	Arthur	Truman	Murphy	Sammy	Jack	Fig
1981								
1982	↓							
1983	│	│						
1984	│	│						
1985	│	│						
1986	│	│						
1987	│	│						
1988	│	│						
1989	│	│						
1990	│	│						
1991	│	│						
1992	│	│						
1993	│	│	↓					
1994	│	│						
1995	│	↓						
1996	│							
1997	↓							
1998		│						
1999		│			│			
2001		│			│			
2002		│			│			
2003		│			│			
2004		│			↓			
2005		│						
2006		│				↓		
2007		↓						
2008								
2009					↓			│
2010								│
2011								│
2013								↓

*The years they were in my life

One-third of Fort Bend County was under water when Sauks, Andy, and I left Sugar Land and the greater Houston area the first Saturday in June. In what became known as the Memorial Day Flood of 2016, the rain had been unrelenting. Everything was soggy, the humidity oppressive, and the bugs unlike anything I'd experienced before. For the first time in the nearly thirty years I'd called Texas's swampy Gulf Coast home, I hired an exterminator to get rid of the giant flying beasts Texans call tree or wood roaches.

I'd grown accustomed to one or two making their way indoors and promptly meeting their fate at the paws and jaws of the cats, but now they were invading in hoards too numerous for Sauks and Andy bother with.

In sum, I couldn't wait to get to the high desert mountains of New Mexico.

Both Sauks and Andy hovered nervously nearby while I packed up my Honda CRV, knowing I was leaving but not yet aware they were going with me. While employed I was often on the road, either for business or vacation. I love to travel and my penchant for extending a business trip to include a bit of sightseeing no doubt contributed to the end of my career. I was careful to cover all bases on the work front and never billed the company a dime for any extra expense, but it was still noted with some consternation. The men I worked with had wives, children, and/or other obligations at home, or simply lacked my sense of adventure. So more than one complained. How dare I go to Machu Picchu, the Greek Isles, or even Bryce Canyon rather than head straight back home after wrapping up business?

The first of the two frothing-at-the-mouth bosses that signaled the beginning of the end of my career accused me of flitting off on a Kenyan safari without filing any copy. No, I replied through gritted teeth, I worked hard on a cover piece on the conference I'd attended in Nairobi and made sure it was letter perfect and published before "flitting off" to Amboseli, a national park in the shadows of Kilimanjaro renowned for its herds of elephants.

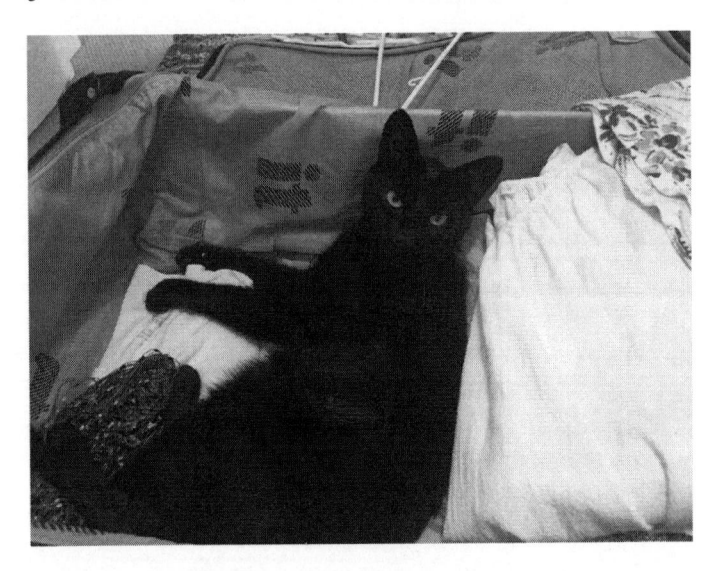

So Sauks and Andy know the drill. They note with alarm when a suitcase is pulled out of a closet and watch uneasily as I pack, occasionally jumping in with the clothes in an attempt to hinder my progress.

I've had Sauks long enough he's endured two prolonged absences. In the heartbreaking years after Mike died, I worked back-to-back summers in Geneva, Switzerland. The first, I was so homesick for the cats I nearly didn't return for the second. It was one of the reasons I was more than content to trade Europe for the American West in 2016. With no international borders to cross and a drivable route, I could bring them along.

Each of those summers abroad, I found house sitters who took good care of the cats and the homestead. The first couple told me

Sauks and Fig, one of the cats I've since lost, were very distraught when they were packing up prior to my return.

They tried to reassure them. "Don't worry. Anne is on her way home."

A few hours later, after nearly missing my connection in Newark while fretting I might have to spend yet-another night without the cats, I burst through the door yelling "Kitties!" They both came running. It is a routine I've followed ever since, generally with the same result, although sadly without Fig.

Fig while still a resident of J-Canine

Ah, Fig. That is probably as good a strand as any to start with as I try to unravel in my tangled yarn of love and loss. She was an orange tabby, which alone made her special as only 15 percent of gingers—as they are known in the British Isles—are female. Someone had dropped her off when she was a half-grown kitten at the kennel Mike and I used when we were out of town As Joni, the owner of the J-Canine Pet Resort noted, when an animal's boarding fee reached one thousand dollars and the owner no longer picked up the phone, she knew it had been abandoned. Joni named these animals (both dogs and cats) alphabetically, so Fig was the sixth to meet such a fortuitous fate.

I remember clearly the first time I saw Fig. She was sitting in the window of Joni's cattery, which is in a bucolic setting beyond Rosenberg on the outer most ring of Houston.

"Oh, look at the ginger cat," I exclaimed.

I'd developed a fondness for gingers after Mike brought one into my life. Jack was an inner-city, dumpster scavenger who'd lived on the rather-rough streets surrounding Mike's bachelor pad. There are different shades of orange cats, ranging from a deep pumpkin to wheat colored, and Jack was on the light end of that scale. The first time I saw him he was a small, tawny tiger curled on Mike's doormat, much the same color as the ground ginger used in holiday baking. Fig, on the other hand, was a bit rosier, not orange as much as a light shade of auburn.

Jack in Sugar Land

As cats are wont to do, Jack adopted Mike. It started when Mike's downstairs neighbors asked him to feed a stray kitten they'd named Jack when they were away. These neighbors eventually moved and Jack turned to Mike. Since Mike was a dog person by upbringing, the process was slow but steady. First a steady meal, then occasional access to his apartment, then a nap on his bed and, finally, overnight privileges. After that, Mike left a window ajar so Jack could come and go as he pleased. But being a dog person, Mike never went so far as to invest in a litter box. If Jack found his window access blocked, he simply went to the door and, like a dog, asked to be let out.

Jack, along with Mike, eventually made his way to my house in the relatively posh Houston suburbs. I still blame Jack's ensuing diabetes on his new, cushy life. Fancy Feast was probably a shock to his system after a diet of mice and rats and table scraps foraged out of trash cans. When first diagnosed, Jack needed daily insulin shots.

15

Then it was twice a day. That and the danger of insulin shock afterward dictated he be boarded when we were traveling.

Every time we drove through cotton and rice fields to drop Jack off, Joni would try her best to get us to adopt Fig. But we were steadfast: with Jack plus my black cat Sammy, we had more than enough to worry about when we were on the road, which was often.

All of that changed rapidly in the nightmare that began unfolding, aptly enough, on a Friday the 13th in February 2009. This thread is long and twisted, so bear with me.

Mike and I were going to spend the weekend in Austin, combining a Valentine's Day celebration with my sister Susan's participation in the Austin Marathon. Those plans were thwarted when Sammy disappeared. A declawed housecat, he had escaped from the backyard, apparently chased out into the street by our neighbor's dog who had broken through the adjoining fence. Sammy returned within in twenty-four hours, but he had been hit by a car. He succumbed to internal injuries a few days later.

Mike took Sammy's death hard, particularly since the cat had gotten out on his watch. It seemed to

Sammy in the garden.

16

accelerate an ongoing decline in Mike's health, an unknown condition I'd been harping upon for several months. I can only guess why he refused to see a doctor but two weeks later Mike became so ill he ended up in the hospital, alas much too late. The diagnosis was swift and brutal: malignant hypertension. He went into heart failure and passed away on March 4.

Just that quick, I was alone save for Jack. And, that was little comfort as the poor cat had one paw on a banana peel and the other three over a kitty grave. Jack had suffered so many life-threatening insulin crashes I kept a bottle of corn syrup handy on the kitchen table to snap him out of it.

Mike and I once walked in to find Jack delirious and yowling in pain. We laid him out on the kitchen table and I rubbed his tongue and teeth with syrup. Jack went limp and Mike cried out, "You've killed him." Fortunately, not. Within a few moments, Jack shook himself off and shakily got back on his feet.

Now with both Sam and Mike gone and Jack in constant danger, I decided to adopt Fig. Joni and her staff bathed her for her new home, and she arrived smelling—aptly enough—like pumpkin pie. Having spent two years in a cage, she was thrilled to have the run of a three-bedroom house. The kitchen island became her domain after she made a running leap and skated across it, sending coffee mugs flying into a glass-top table. Despite her wild, destructive streak, Fig was extremely affectionate, becoming the only true lap cat I've ever had. She knew the one time I could be counted upon to sit still was when the television was on, so flipping on the remote always brought her running to the sofa.

And that's where we ended up two months to the day after Mike's departure, when Jack decided to join him in the great beyond. I probably went through two bottles of wine and three boxes of Kleenex while blindly channel surfing. It's not a pretty way to mourn, but rather my version of keening and renting one's clothes. In other words, by this point I'd resorted to doing whatever it takes to get through the raw grief of the first day. Losing a pet, which is such a solitary experience, accommodates this messy approach. If you've got friends and family present, you not only have other shoulders to lean upon but also the incentive to not to make a spectacle of yourself. But after Jack's death, it was just Fig and me. She curled in a ball in my lap and purred, doing her best to provide comfort as I slugged down enough wine to stay numb and stared at random movies through tear-blurred eyes.

A few days later Sauks came into the picture. This gray-and-white tuxedo cat was a gift from my long-time pet sitter. It takes a special kind of animal person to say, "Anne, you've been through so much let me give you my cat." But that's precisely what happened.

After Sammy and Mike's death, I'd enlisted Tamorra to check on Jack while I was at work. It was her job to make sure he'd eaten rather than sleeping the day away as is the nature of housecats and then go into insulin shock. Assigned with this task and fully aware of why, she was well acquainted with my three consecutive losses.

Sauks had been just a tiny kitten when Tamorra had spied him on the side of the road outside Needville, another farming community just southwest of Houston. He was now two years old and living in and out of her garage because her daughter was allergic to him.

"He deserves a better life" Tamorra said as she handed him over, a bulky thirteen pounds, along with his medical records. That's when I discovered she had misspelled his name.

"I'm a bit dyslexic," she explained, laughing.

I don't know why I didn't change it, except I can't claim to have been thinking too clearly myself at the time.

Sauks and Fig hit it off instantly. They playfully chased each other around the house, cuddled like litter mates, and regularly groomed each other. So, while the occupants of my house had completely rotated in a short span of three months and I was just beginning to feel the full extent of my losses, I had the companionship and comfort of two very content felines.

I was lucky with Fig and Sauks as dynamics between cats can be tricky. Although generally social animals, sometimes they cannot stand each other for no discernible reason. Such was the case with Murphy and Sammy. Murphy and I had been left alone when my first black cat, Arthur, and Don died within a month of each other, much like the situation I found myself in a dozen years later when Sammy, Mike, and Jack departed this life. I knew I'd be traveling and, therefore, adopted Sammy from a local rescue league to keep Murphy company. It didn't go well. To the end of her days, Murphy hated him, standing on her hind legs to box his ears anytime his path crossed hers. I should add that Murphy did not take well to Mike entering our lives either. She was truly a one-person cat.

Murphy pissed at Mike as usual

So, with the camaraderie between Sauks and Fig, I didn't even think about adopting another cat until I saw Andy. I was no more looking for a kitten than another husband, but then I might be married again if I'd come across an available human male specimen as perfect as this sleek black kitten.

Looking at kittens in pet stores has long been a therapy for me. Back in the 1990s when I was subjected to the wrath of a good-old-boy boss who hated my smart-alecky Yankee ass, I often comforted myself with a visit to a long-defunct pet store in the Galleria basement. Now, it is a swing through the pet adoption center either at PetsMart or Petco while buying cat food.

True I am often tempted (I still remember a pair of orange kittens named Mango and Tango I had to tear myself away from), but so far I have held steadfast to my vow to never become a crazy cat lady opposed to a normal, run-of-the-mill cat lady. The breaking point, in my opinion, is three cats, a limit I occasionally hit but have yet to exceed. And that was the case when I came across three-month-old Andy.

Despite losing two black cats just days before the deaths of my two husbands (talk about bad luck), I still love black cats. More than ginger cats like Jack and Fig? More than fluffy brown tabbies like Murphy? Hard to say, but it is well documented that black cats in particular need homes. Sure enough there was a sign on Andy's cage declaring that all his siblings had been adopted and now it was his turn. This was a kitten I could not walk away from.

He was glossy black without a single white hair. (Arthur and Sammy had a few white hairs in identical spots on their chests and bellies.) His up-tilted eyes were changeable in color, ranging from copper to emerald depending on his surroundings and mood. He liked to cuddle, cozying up to any cat or human who would tolerate him. And someone had given him the unfortunate name of Dandy. Even at three months, he seemed to know his name, so I just dropped the D.

Andy has been a blessing and a curse. The adoption agency neutered him before I took him home, which I believe is the reason he's relatively small for a male cat. He's a bit heavier after his summer on the road, much of which was first confined to our tiny casita in New Mexico and then a single bedroom here and there, but still svelte. And now that he's fully grown, it is evident from his meow to his triangular face to his out-sized personality and playfulness that he has a strong strain of Siamese blood. Those are the blessings.

The curse is that I suspect Andy had a hand in Fig's demise. He upset the balance between Fig and Sauks, inserting himself between the two like a jealous, youngest sibling. Within moments of letting

22

Andy loose just inside the door, Sauks rolled across the room with Andy a tiny black appendage on his belly.

In the following weeks Sauks, chubby due to his kitten-hood addiction to Purina's Delicat (aka Delifat, which it took some effort to break), lost a full pound jousting with the ever-demanding Andy. Fig, on the other hand, couldn't be bothered, retreating to become a rather sad and solitary animal.

A year later, the every-playful Andy kept pouncing on Fig as she continued to lose weight and otherwise fail. Despite the two-grand-plus I spent trying to determine what was wrong with her, Fig wasted away. It was only in the post-mortem that I learned she tested positive for Feline Infectious Peritonitis, the first case my vet had seen in a decade.

I didn't think I could cry harder than I had for Jack, but there was a bit of comfort in no longer struggling to keep him alive. There was no such straw to grasp with the loss of Fig. We spent her last night together in my home office, away from the other two cats. I slept fitfully on the daybed, while she cried and looked for places to hide as cats want nothing more than to be alone at the end. I feared she wouldn't make it through the night. At first light, I wrapped her in a towel and took her back to the vet—where she'd undergone many tests in the preceding weeks—to have her put down. I was crying so hard that he told me to walk out and come back later to settle the bill.

It occurred to me later that Fig was a gift granted to me to get past Mike. She had served her purpose and was taken from me four years later. That meant it was time for me to move on.

So, my household had shrunk back to me and two cats.

In early June 2016, the three of us hit the road. While on our journey, we were occasionally joined by the ghosts of my past loves.

Chapter 2: Leaving Sugar Land

June 3: Sugar Land to Silverton, Texas; 565 miles

Listening to a cardinal sing, wondering when I'd hear that bird again, I packed the CRV with two suitcases of clothing, camping and hiking gear, my mountain bike, a bag of books I somehow never got around to reading, my computer, and the kitty condo. Don and I bought this three-foot-high carpeted cylinder a lifetime ago in Denver for Arthur, the black cat whose death preceded Don's by a month. It has been in constant use by a succession of cats ever since.

I threw the kitty condo in the car thinking it would help Sauks and Andy acclimate to their new home in New Mexico, which it did, but it also proved useful on the road. In the nearly 5,000 miles we racked up, Sauks preferred the floor or the center console, but Andy spent 90 percent of his time holed up in it like an owl in a hollow tree trunk.

When the CRV was packed, I grabbed the cats, shoved them into carriers and deposited them in the front seat. Their alert level had escalated from orange to red when I shut the bedroom doors to prevent them from taking cover under the beds. Now, both were thoroughly pissed off. Andy was particularly uncooperative, so I had to resort to putting the carrier on its end and strong-arming him in head first.

Even as a lifelong cat owner, the amount of strength these creatures cram into ten or fifteen pounds still astounds me. It once took Don, who was six-four and athletic, and me every bit of brute force we could summon to give our Siamese cat Truman a flea bath. In the end, we were drenched head to foot and every available towel was heaped in a sodden island in the lake now covering the bathroom floor.

Once I'd wrestled the devils into the car, I realized I needed to fill the gas tank. But I wanted to give Sauks and Andy a chance to settle in first and waited until the fuel light came on about an hour up the road in Navasota. By this time, both cats were roaming free. It is admittedly dangerous, but I defy anyone to drive eight hours or so while listening to two cats yowl in their carriers.

As I squeezed out the door at the Shell station, Sauks made an earnest attempt to follow. Fortunately, that was the exception rather than the norm. While each and every exit and entrance from the car in the following months was made with extreme caution, followed by an OCD check to make sure both were still present, few escapes were attempted.

As a cat lover, I've gleaned a whole repertoire of heart-warming kitty stories (and some dreadful ones I'll try not to share) over the years. One of the most poignant, probably long forgotten by everyone save the original party and me, was of a kitten lost at a gas station. This story, told second or third hand, was of a young couple and their newly acquired kitten making the journey from Denver back to visit the family farm in North Dakota. They stopped for gas, perhaps in the middle of the night (recent college graduates rarely have money for motels) and somehow their kitten got out of the car. After an indeterminate amount of fruitless searching, they went on their way heartbroken.

On the way back to Denver, they stopped at the same station just for the sake of trying, and miracle of miracles: the kitten was there waiting for them. Even with this happy ending, I can still feel everyone's pain: the pall hanging over what was supposed to be a happy family gathering while a terrified kitten survived against the odds, dodging a steady stream of cars and trucks stopping to fill up.

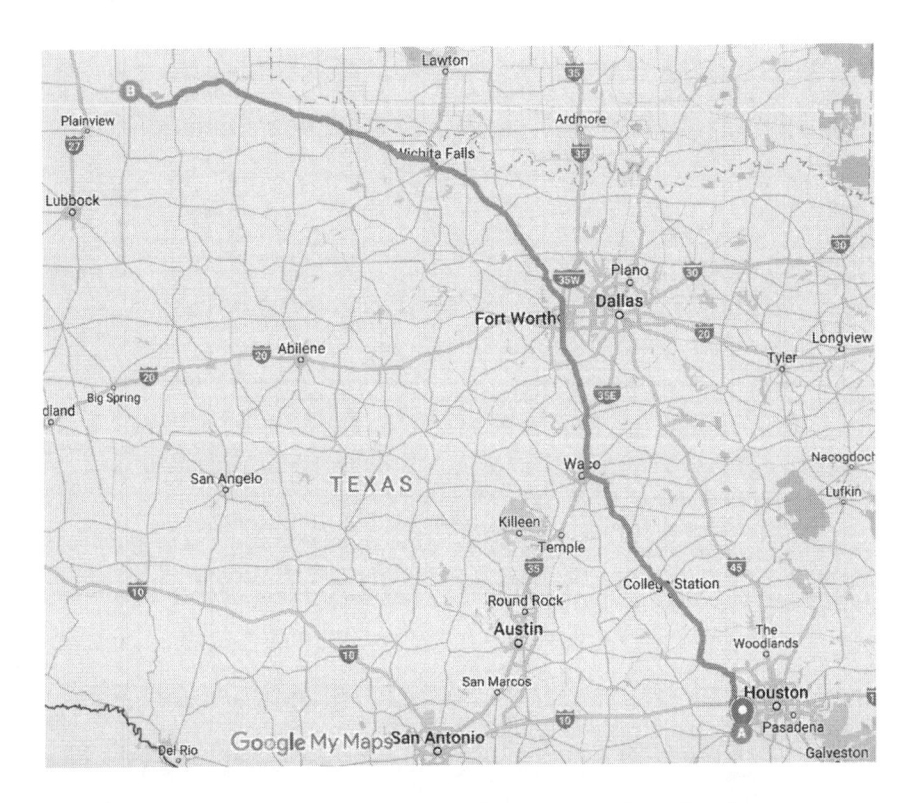

With a tankful of gas, we got back on the road. Destination: Silverton, Texas. I'd always wanted to hike the canyon lands of the Texas Panhandle and with a bit of Internet searching had found a cabin about twenty miles from Caprocks State Park. If I hadn't had the cats, I would have camped. I love camping and long ago, when I was young and even crazier than I am now, I actually camped with a cat on numerous occasions in Colorado. Now just the thought of a cat in a tent makes me shudder. It won't happen again as long as I've still got the money to put a roof over our heads.

In addition to vetoing the idea of camping with cats, I'd decided not to stop and see an old friend in North Texas as originally planned. If losing my job wasn't painful enough, I'd also managed to have my heart broken a month earlier. When Mike, who truly was the love of my life, died it destroyed something intangible inside of me; after a while I could no longer feel it but men could spot it a mile away. Call it a widow's aura or what you will, but one man after another rebuffed me on many an encounter, blind date or otherwise.

As luck would have it, when the spell was finally broken I fell madly in love with someone I knew from the start would leave me. Better to have loved and lost will probably be my epitaph. So, when mapping out my trip to New Mexico for yet-another cure, I figured a first step in recovery might be an evening of laughter with someone who'd been carrying a torch for me for a long time. If it went further than that, so be it.

But once on the road, I quickly reconsidered. I called my friend as I whizzed past Wichita Falls at eighty-miles-plus-per-hour.

"I'm sorry," I explained. "I figure you, me, two bottles of wine, two cats, and an eight-year-old," he was babysitting his grandson, "are a sure recipe for disaster."

We traded a bit of flirtatious banter and agreed to try again in the not-so-distant future. Then I was on the high plains of northwest Texas for the first time in more than a dozen years.

In my first decade in Houston, this drive was an annual summer pilgrimage. The move to Texas was a last-ditch effort to save my marriage to Don. Instead, it just prolonged its death throes. Deeply in debt, watching Don slowly drink himself to death, I buried myself in my career and looked forward to summer when I'd escape alone to Colorado for ten days or so.

The country opens up northwest of Fort Worth on US Route 287 and for me it feels like going home. I grew up on a farm in northeastern Nebraska and most summers we would make our way west on family road trips to Colorado. Our spirits would rise as the cornfields thinned and the horizon expanded until the blue line of the Rockies appeared in the distance.

Then after graduating (barely) from the University of Nebraska, I moved to Denver since it was the easiest escape route from the plowed ground of the northern plains. I had a passionate love affair with the mountains and if it had not been for Don's persuasion, I would never have left. And while Houston has been one of the best things to ever happen to me in many ways, giving me both Mike and a career in the international sector, crossing the hundredth meridian heading west always gives me a high.

That is perhaps the reason why I have a certain fondness for Childress, which lies just a few miles west of the hundredth. Beyond Wichita Falls, US 287 runs west-northwest paralleling the Red River a dozen or so miles to the north. The Red River is the Oklahoma border until the boundary makes a sharp right turn at the hundredth meridian, forming the eastern side of the Texas Panhandle. Meanwhile US 287 continues its northwesterly journey.

Childress, with a population of about 6,000, has a bit of movie history. It was the location of the nearest phone in the original *The*

Texas Chain Saw Massacre. It is also the home of Jack Twist played by Jake Gyllenhaal in *Brokeback Mountain.* Neither movie was actually filmed there. This is also the case with the 2016 western *Hell or High Water.* Once again Childress is mentioned, but the movie was filmed across the state line in New Mexico. That explains the occasional backdrop of mountains on the far horizon. The only mountains in Texas are more than 300 miles southwest of Childress.

I hardly slowed down while driving through Childress, which was always the end of my first day while driving between Houston and Colorado. I'd stay at the Best Western, which then seemed to be the only decent hotel between Wichita Falls and Amarillo. I noted that it is now the Red Roof Inn and has been joined by three or four new hotels. It seems things are looking up for Childress.

K-Bob's Steakhouse, where I once ate one of the best steaks ever off a plastic plate in the glare of a salad bar with a large selection of multi-colored Jell-O, was still there. I had desperately wanted a glass of red wine to go with that prime cut of beef, but alas Childress County was dry. (A quick Google search indicates that is no longer the case; it seems the town now even has a winery. As I said, things are apparently looking up for Childress.) I also noted a Thai restaurant. Years ago on a return trip to Houston, I ate Thai leftovers from Vail heated up in the microwave of my Best Western room. I figured I was probably the first ever to enjoy that particular cuisine in that town.

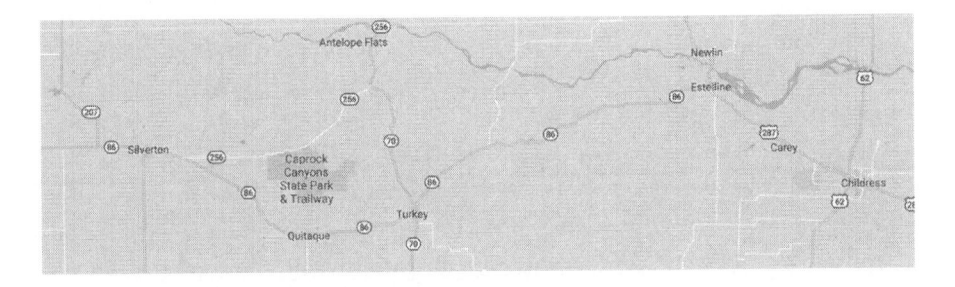

I had another hour's drive ahead of me. Sauks and Andy were by now resigned to their fate and quietly tucked away. I turned off US 287 at Estelline, just before it crosses the Prairie Dog Fork of the Red River, and made the last fifty-seven miles on one of those narrow, undulating two-lane blacktops I've come to love in Texas. I met maybe a half dozen cars. After crossing the narrow escarpment that runs north and south through this part of Texas, I was back on table-top flat farm land.

Silverton was so tiny I was through it before I had time to consider where my cabin might be. I made a left-hand turn at the last cross street and looked for a place to turn around. As fortune would have it, that just so happened to be my destination: Silver Winds RV Park and Cabins. I opened the car door to one of my favorite sounds in the world; the day had begun with a serenade of cardinals and was now ending with the evening song of western meadowlarks.

After checking in, I pulled up to the porch of my cabin to make the first of many cat transfers. Since Sauks was handy, I stuffed his furry thirteen pounds into a carrier, hustled him inside, and let him loose.

I figured I could handle Andy without the carrier and he cooperatively curled into a tight ball in my arms. Once inside, both took cover. Since the beds (I'd requested one, but there were three crammed into the tiny room) were on platforms, they crouched as close to those platforms as possible, getting some shelter from the overhanging bedspreads. Meanwhile, I transported their food and litter box before attending to my own needs, which consisted mostly of a glass of wine to shake off the road.

This became a routine I perfected in the coming months. After a while, I no longer bothered with carrier for either Sauks or Andy. And I really came to appreciate those platform beds because there are few things more annoying than trying to pry a cat out from underneath a bed.

Chapter 3: My first day in the west

June 4: Silverton and Caprocks Canyon State Park

"Do you know where the trail is?"

I'd caught up with the two young men who'd passed me on the approach to the rocky bluff we were now perched on, about half way up. The trail map had labeled this portion of the hike as extremely steep and rugged, with the advisory that you climbed cliffs and bluffs at your own risk. I'd had a hard time believing that, but now that I was making the climb, sometimes hand over hand, I knew what they meant. And the trail was nearly impossible to follow.

"Beats me," I said. A glance upward told me we were not even close. But where?

"Wow. Look at your hiking boots."

I glanced at their tattered running shoes.

There are advantages to being old, money being a primary one. I'd bought my boots a year earlier in Santa Fe. A trendy shoe store in the middle of town had several pairs marked 50 percent off, which put them in my price range.

"Do you have these in a seven?" I'd asked, holding up a boot for the clerk to see.

"No," he replied curtly, turning to assist two women who apparently appeared "better heeled."

"Then how about this one?" I asked after he'd delivered several pairs to his other customers.

"You don't give up, do you?"

Despite his rudeness, I bought a pair of Patagonia's and broke them in on hikes just outside Santa Fe. Or at least I thought I did. But they tore up my feet when I went to Big Bend National Park just a couple weeks after being "made redundant," which is the polite British term for the ugly act of taking one's job away. A week later I'd had to apologize to my lover for the terrible condition of my feet. Fortunately, he was an outdoorsman so we'd compared callouses. Alas, I won this dubious competition hands down due to my oozing blisters.

"Yeah, I got these boots after retiring a well-worn pair in the Canadian Rockies last year," I told my fellow hikers. "Where you from?"

Both were students at Texas Tech in Lubbock, which explained their worn shoes. We agreed to try different directions in search of the trail. They headed up to the left, while I retreated down to the right. That was when I spotted a trail marker a bit below me.

"This way." I yelled back at them.

Once on top. I paused to take in the view. Several hikers passed me. Some were going on to Fern Cave, others doing the entire loop. I was turning around here because I was nervous about Sauks and Andy back in our cabin where I'd left the windows open for their enjoyment. The screens were tight and they seemed content, but I was still a bit paranoid. This would become another common theme of our summer.

I needn't have worried. When I returned, both were sleepily stretched out on the beds. Except for transfers to and from the car and a bit of meowing on Sauks's part for the first few miles of any day's driving, they were exceptional travelers—at least for cats.

While on the road, Sauks and Andy went into something of a hibernation mode, requiring neither food nor drink. Of the thirteen days on the road, only once was the litter box used and that was an early morning pee by Sauks on one of our first days. After that, he apparently knew to use the bathroom before we got on the road.

I'd experienced this phenomenon decades earlier when I'd made my way to San Diego after spending Christmas in Nebraska with the traveler cat of all traveler cats, Hershey, a chocolate-point Siamese I'd acquired my first year out of college. I left the family farm with Hershey at dawn, drove a hundred miles south to Omaha, stopped to visit a friend, and then spent four hours in the airport waiting for a snowed-in flight from Chicago.

Upon arrival at LAX, Hershey and I met my boyfriend who was kind enough drive us to San Diego since we had missed our connecting flight. Before getting in the car, I let the poor cat out on a patch of packed earth outside the terminal in case he needed to relieve himself. He put up his nose in disgust, so we threw him in the car to make the final 125 miles down the 405 and I-5 freeways. Arriving back at my apartment about two hours later, Hershey finally deigned to eat, drink, and use the litter box. That trip took fifteen hours.

During the summer of 2016, Sauks, Andy, and I traveled in stretches ranging from a mere seventy miles to a whopping 657 miles. The average for our 13 days on the road was 365 miles and only two of those days were for less than one hundred miles. I stopped for many bathroom breaks, but Sauks and Andy had no such needs.

Chapter 4: Crossing the state line

June 5: Silverton, Texas, to Tijeras, New Mexico; 346 miles

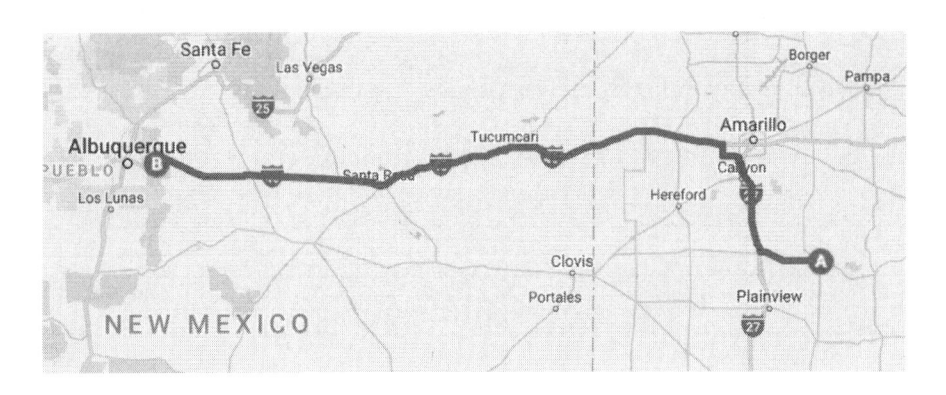

I found Artista Casita Del Sol Sunny Mellow on Airbnb. Nearly everything about it was perfect: the location in the Sandia Mountains just outside of Albuquerque, the price that included a discount of more than 50 percent for a monthly booking, and the grounds that featured a lavender garden, vineyard, fruit orchard, and vegetable patch. Most importantly, it was pet friendly and the owners didn't flinch when I confessed I was bringing two cats.

My only concern was its size. From the photos I could tell it was essentially one room that had been divided into three spaces: a kitchen/living area, a bedroom, and a bathroom. Bedroom was a bit of a misnomer since there was no wall let alone a door between it and the kitchen. And the space was so small the double bed was shoved up against the wall. The bathroom was separate, but had a curtain rather than a door that closed let alone latched.

These weren't obstacles I couldn't easily overcome. The objective of this trip was to spend as much time as possible outside anyway. My concern was the cats. They were used to having the run of a 2,000-square-foot house, where at least once a day Andy would tear through the house like his tail was on fire. How would we all cope in such a tiny space?

I am a typical cat person in that I can completely tune out both Sauks and Andy's attempts to get my attention. On occasion, I've only noticed one of them is on my desk when they either step on the keyboard or shove their butt right in my face. At the kitchen table, they can count on me finally acknowledging their presence by sitting on the newspaper or magazine I'm attempting to read. All other efforts—meowing, pawing at my face, purring—tend to fail.

Such was the case when Andy was still a kitten. I was working on an early morning deadline when I noticed that Andy was dashing back and forth across the room trilling—that lovely combination of purring and meowing. His attempts to get my attention finally worked; Andy and I still play a bit of tag around the house.

Andy isn't the only cat I've played tag with. Murphy would come into the bedroom when I was getting ready to turn in, meow and then run back out into the darkened house. When I finally caught on to this game, I'd invariably find her behind the desk in my office. With the lights out, it was the darkest nook in the house.

Ah, Murphy. I credit her with saving my marriage to Don (if you can call sticking it out until the bitter end "saving it"). And when Don was gone, she became my closest companion. That was also Jack's role in Mike's life. He was an extraordinarily intelligent cat, and took to reminding Mike to get off the damned computer and give him his insulin shot by repeatedly coming into the office and meowing. Just like when Murphy tried to get me to chase her, Mike didn't catch on at first. Jack had food and water. Catnip didn't satisfy him. So what was it? Then it dawned on Mike: it was time for Jack's injection.

I packed up the car in Silverton wondering just how Sauks and Andy were going to take to a new, severely restricted space. Well, it was time to find out. The cabin we were leaving was even tinier than our destination, which doesn't mean they didn't give it an all-out feline effort to hide when they realized they were about to be thrown back in the car.

Sauks took to the space between the bed and wall, as far back as possible, forcing me onto my hands and knees in a very confined space. Andy made it a bit easier, simply crawling under the covers. He quickly learned this was futile and never tried that ploy again, although in the ensuing weeks on the road he did stump me once by taking shelter behind a pillow.

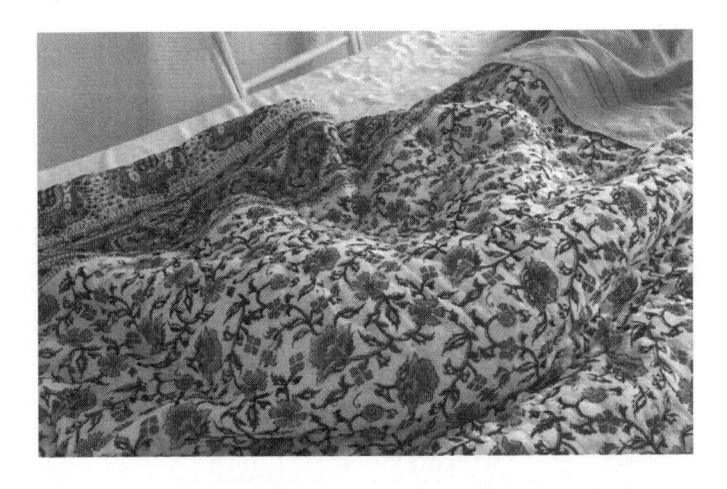

It was all to no avail. The three of us were on the road by mid-morning, anticipating a mid-afternoon arrival. I drove west to Interstate 27 and then north to Amarillo, where I got on I-40. I would be spending the next two months just over the hill from I-40, much of which parallels Route 66. I crossed into New Mexico at the ghost town of Glenrio. The next time I would drive across the Texas state line would be thirteen weeks and two days later and more than five hundred miles to the east on the other end of the state.

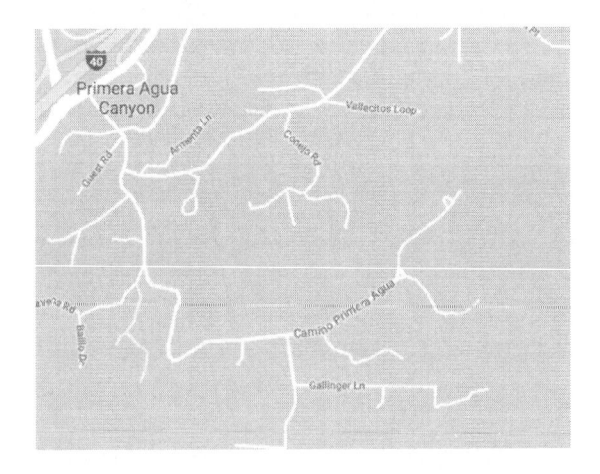

While on the road I got a notification from my Airbnb host that my casita was ready. The directions on how to get there were long and complex for what turned out to be an easy route: the first two lefts off I-40 and then an immediate right. It was the meandering drive up and over the hill that took up most of the text, when just following Camino Primera Agua Road until turns east into a mountain valley—easy to do with a GPS—got me where I wanted to go. I nearly missed the driveway, but recognized the casita and vineyard from the web photos. We were home.

Sauks and Andy fell asleep on the bed while I was still unpacking. My hosts had turned on the window air-conditioning unit on for my comfort. Relishing the warm, dry mountain air, I switched it off and opened the three windows and the double front door. I noted the screen doors weren't particularly tight and wondered how long it would take the cats to figure that out.

In the next couple weeks, I began to suspect Sauks and Andy were, like me, having a hard time adjusting to the altitude. Tijeras, which is Spanish for scissors, sits above 6,000 feet. They seemed to sleep more than usual, if that was possible. And they drank an extraordinary amount of water.

Housecats are descended from wild desert cats native to North Africa and the Middle East and therefore are notoriously finicky about drinking water. Scientists attribute to this to the fact their ancestors had little access to fresh water and got most of their fluids from eating prey. I'd found out by accident that Sauks prefers his water with ice presented on the kitchen island. It serves a dual purpose since not only does he eagerly lap it up but he has to stay fit enough to get up there. Shortly after that discovery I read on the internet that cats do not like their water bowl anywhere near their food, presumably due to an innate fear of contamination. It took me how many decades of cat ownership to find this out?

In New Mexico finding a spot for their water proved a bit of a challenge since there was hardly any kitchen counter space, let alone an island. The perfect solution proved to be a glass of water on the dresser in the bathroom. This was a spot often visited by Sauks and Andy since it accessed the bathroom window, which was their favorite of the three in the casita because it looked out on a bird feeder. In the next two months they'd spend hours there watching the towhees and finches.

The other two windows also kept them happily occupied. The kitchen window looked out over the vineyard. Since my quarters were so small, I'd eat dinner under that arbor, usually with Andy serenading me with insistent cries from the kitchen window.

The third window was above the bed. This meant my sleep was often disturbed when one of the cats jumped down, not bothering to avoid my prone figure. Unfortunately, that was also where Andy was sitting one day when he had a violent reaction to Sheba's beef pâté. His projectile vomiting resulted in a dark brown goo sprayed all over the bed that, to paraphrase Dave Chapelle, looked good and poopy. Check out Chapelle's Popcopy skit on YouTube if I haven't painted a graphic enough picture.

I promptly stripped the bed and hung the sheets outside in the near-zero percent humidity of mid-afternoon. Within a half an hour they were dry enough to scrape off the ugly mess before tossing them in the wash. I swore off Sheba beef pâté once and for all, hauling the remaining cans all the way back to Houston where I fed it to a feral cat I was trying to tame. I figure the poor creature probably had a much less delicate stomach than spoiled-rotten Andy. And if it did happen to disagree with him, well he barfed it up somewhere far outside my house.

But all this drama was in our future at this point. After unpacking, I ran to the nearest grocery store for a few items. Google maps revealed a market three miles up New Mexico Highway 14. My new summer home sat at the southern terminus of this back route to Santa Fe, which is also known as the Turquoise Trail. I'd taken this road, which meanders along the eastern side of the Sandias, any number of times on earlier trips through New Mexico. Now I would get to know the very southern stretch between I-40 and Sandia Crest Road quite well indeed.

While scoping out the map, I also noted Burger Boy was the nearest restaurant, assuming Molly's Bar just down the hill didn't have any food beyond Beer Nuts.

Burger Boy doesn't sound promising, I thought. Its appearance wasn't much more inviting, but I did notice all the cars in the lot and decided to give it a try nonetheless. I ate many green chili burgers over the next two months, but none nearly as good as those I scarfed down in the shade of a pine tree overlooking the Turquoise Trail at Burger Boy.

My first day in Tijeras ended with a mountain shower. It took me a moment or two to identify the source of the sudden loud pinging: the casita had a tin roof that amplified the sound of falling rain. The scent of lavender and other desert vegetation I had yet to identify saturated. In the coming weeks, I'd have to relearn all that I'd once known about mountain weather.

That first rain must have been some sort of housewarming gift because thereafter those afternoon showers were few and far between, even after monsoon season "began" in July.

Part 2: Tijeras, New Mexico, June 5-July 31

Chapter 5: Staking Out Our New Territory

The cats and I spent the remainder of June and all of July in Tijeras. Or at least Sauks and Andy did while I made several short road trips, traveling up to Colorado twice, camping with my nephew near Angel Fire in northern New Mexico one weekend, and meeting an old college friend in Flagstaff.

Artista Casita Del Sol Sunny Mellow

Fortunately, Andy and Sauks got to stay "home" since my hostess at Casita Del Sol was the perfect pet sitter. Their Airbnb listing had a wide array of photos and as an itinerant traveler, I spent a fair amount of time looking at them. I noted that the couple that owned the place were blond and quite attractive.

I met Robbie the very first day. Since writing was a top priority and I needed to keep looking for work, the Internet was essential and I couldn't seem to sign on. A quick call brought Robbie down from the "big house."

"If you need anything," she explained while rebooting the server (why hadn't I tried that), "call me not Gregory. I'm the one who gets things done around here."

Robbie was delightful to have around, and she instantly took to Sauks and Andy, and vice versa. She had two pets, Bentley, a small white dog she'd walk early in the morning, and Marlena, a fluffy cat named after Marlene Dietrich due to a black spot on her cheek.

During one of our first mornings the very elegant Marlena came to visit. Back in Texas the appearance of a cat in our yard causes an eruption of yowling and growling on both Sauks and Andy's part. In New Mexico, they seemed to know they were guests and just calmly observed from the window. This held true for both Marlena and a neighborhood cat that visited regularly from across the road.

Robbie tried to keep Marlena indoors as much as possible due to the abundance of wildlife in the area. On one of my last nights in Tijeras, I made my way back to the casita from the "big house" long after dark. Before leaving, Gregory teased me that they were not to be held liable for any attacks by bears or mountain lions, both of which lived nearby.

Fortunately, I saw neither. There were signs posted in town instructing to not put the trash out in advance because of bears. But Robbie said the bears didn't come down from the mountain valleys during the summer. She amended that somewhat when I fixed the bird bath behind the casita. It consisted of a homemade wooden stand and plastic pot bottom. When I tried to fill it, I found the "basin" was cracked and picked up a replacement for a couple dollars.

"The bears keep coming down for water and breaking those," Robbie noted.

Fortunately, it didn't happen on my watch.

I did hear coyotes nearly every night, often at dawn, and once as late as nine in the morning. Sometimes they sounded like they were in the pasture right across the road. Sauks and Andy apparently have no survival instincts left, even though each is more than likely just one generation removed from being feral (as are most rescue cats), because they didn't flick an ear.

On the other hand, Andy went into full, puffed-up alert when a deer happened to stroll through our yard. I laughed as he ran from window to window in a panic.

Really? A deer, Andy? With all those wild canines out there that would tear you limb from limb, you're afraid of a deer?

I know very little of Andy's beginnings. I'm assuming he was born in someone's back yard, but perhaps not as he's never had the least bit of interest in going outside (except a few weeks hence in New Mexico, a story I'll share later).

Sauks is a different story. As I've mentioned, he was found on the side of the road as a kitten and then spent a year or two as an indoor/outdoor cat. He is quite the escape artist and must be closely watched when doors are opened. That said, I'm assuming he has enough street smarts to survive for an hour or two outside.

Fig, like Andy, had no experience as an outdoor cat that I knew of. Once she and Sauks knocked out a window screen and I found them some time later in the side yard. Fig was snooping around while Sauks sat on the fence above, apparently acting as her sentinel.

Andy also once escaped through a loose screen. On that occasion, I'd been working late, cleaning up a newsletter created by a recent hire of mine. It was well after eleven o'clock as I'd been on a date earlier that evening and thought this man's work would just need a final check rather than an extensive edit.

I was furious at his sloppiness. He had decades of experience and had been on the job for six weeks and yet the piece was riddled not only with errors in fact, but typos and sentences that ended in mid-air.

At 1 a.m. my eyes crossed and I went to bed, apologizing by email to the morning crew in the UK for leaving the rest of the mess for them to clean up. In my state of anger and frustration, I forgot to shut the office window.

Six hours later, I awoke to the jarring realization of my mistake. My first clue was Sauks curled contently on the foot of the bed, but no sign of Andy.

I ran into my office in a panic.

As I'd feared, the screen was lying on the ground, leaving the window wide open. In the few steps between my office and the front door, I envisioned Andy as nothing more than a furry grease spot on the street.

I flung the door open to a huge, puffy black ball. I picked it up and only after Andy's terror had receded and his fur began to settle back down was I able to determine he was indeed my cat. Sauks came up behind us, not in the least concerned. He'd probably had a calm nightly stroll around the neighborhood before coming back to bed.

Fast forward nearly two years and this far-less-than-adequate employee was retained while I was deemed expendable. I could elaborate on this injustice for pages, but let it suffice to say the report he submitted for publication that evening was not an anomaly. Never in my entire career have I filed an article as flawed as that document. And, that includes pieces I wrote right out of college and the lead story I compiled the day I returned to work in an extremely foggy mental state a week or so after Mike died.

That February morning in 2016 when my vice president walked through the door to tell me I was no longer employed, I had just pushed the publish button after correcting yet-another error-filled article written by the man I was foolish enough to hire.

Amazing how far a pair of testicles and a flair for self-promotion will get one.

Chapter 6: From Flood to Fire

June 23-24: Tijeras, New Mexico, to Salida, Colorado, and back:

Within days of our arrival in Tijeras, a fire broke out a few canyons to the south. How ironic, I thought. I leave an area so flooded I was constantly answering queries from friends and family on whether I was still high and dry and the next thing I know I am facing a forest fire.

Every afternoon, clouds of smoke would billow just above Manzano Mountains visible from my front door. One night the fire was close enough the sky glowed red above the mountains, something I'd not seen since living in Denver.

I followed the news of the Dog Head Fire closely. At first it was thought to have been started by campers, although in the end forest workers and a wood chipper were to blame. The blaze was about fifteen miles away. On a morning drive to hike the nearby Carlito Springs trail, I noticed that the highway leading south out of Tijeras was closed except to local traffic.

None of this concerned me much as I was focused on taking my first jaunt up to Colorado to meet my old college friend. Susie and her husband, Jim, are thinking of retiring in Salida, a small mountain town where they own a rental property. I wondered if I dared ask Robbie to cat sit, but when I did she eagerly agreed.

It was a few days before I was to make the five-hour trip when Gregory stopped to tell me his fire contingency plans.

"I'll cut down these trees," he pointed to the ones between my casita and the road, "as a fire break. We should be okay, but you might want to think about what you'd take if we have to leave on a moment's notice."

That was easy. Purse, jewelry (of more sentimental than monetary value), and the cats. It would be no problem grabbing Andy and carrying him to the car, but Sauks I still wasn't sure about. The casita was so tiny both cat carriers, along with my camping gear, were stored in my car. To facilitate a hasty retreat, I retrieved Sauks's carrier and shoved it under the kitchen table.

Then I began to wonder if I should take Sauks and Andy with me to Salida. It was one thing to ask Robbie to make sure they had food and water. Since it was only an overnight trip, she wouldn't even have to clean the litter box. But trying to round up Sauks and Andy and get them in a vehicle? That was way too much to ask. I took the precaution of booking a pet-friendly motel.

As luck would have it, the fire was pretty much contained by the time I made the first of two drives up through the Rockies that summer, so Sauks and Andy were spared the road trip.

The drive from New Mexico to Colorado through the mountains (as opposed to I-25) to my mind is one of the prettiest in North America.

Early on a Thursday morning in late June, I took the leisurely Turquoise Trail north to Santa Fe. I met few cars and slowed down only to obey the twenty-mile-per-hour speed zone in Madrid, a ghost town turned funky artist colony. My good start came to a grinding halt in the morning rush-hour traffic on US 285 as it follows Saint Francis Drive right through town (I only later discovered the bypass). Then I headed north through mesa country. The highway tracks due east for a few miles through the lush Rio Grande Valley to the hot springs at Ojo Caliente before making a sharp left-hand turn back to the north.

At this point, US 285 travels up through the Carson National

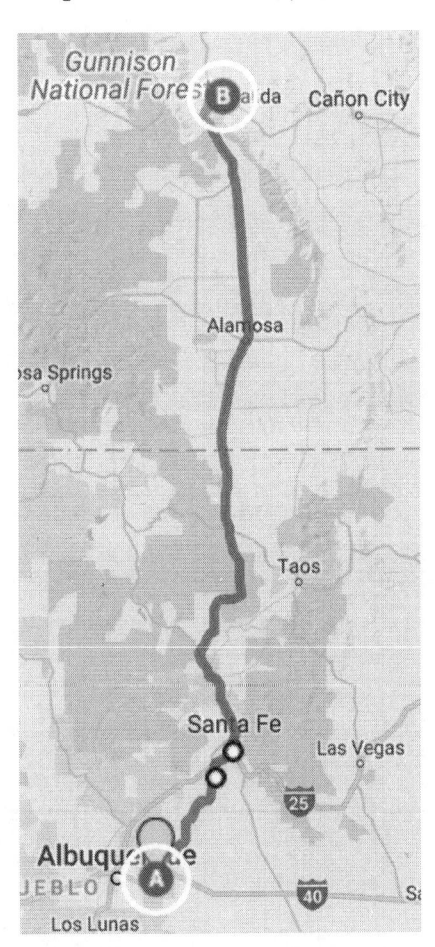

Forest onto a flat volcanic plain dotted with the occasional dormant cone. This federally owned land parallels to the west the Rio Grande del Norte National Monument, which was created by President Obama in 2013.

The 125-mile San Luis Valley begins at Tres Piedres (Three Rocks), about twenty-five miles south of the Colorado state line and some 7,000 feet above sea level. This broad depositional valley lies between the snow-capped San Juan mountains to the west and the Sangre de Cristo mountains to the east. I've heard it called boring, but having lived on a flat coastal plain for nearly three decades I find it quite beautiful.

Once in Salida, I checked into an old motel on the main drag. It was a bit seedy and reminiscent of the many road trips my family made to the mountains when I was a kid. I explained to the gnarly character that ran the front desk that I wouldn't be making the pet deposit as I'd left the cats behind.

"Doesn't matter to me," he shrugged. "I'm just running this place while the owners are out of town."

The next day when I pointed out that I did not have soap in my room and hoped I could borrow a hair drier, I got the same hey-I-don't-really-work-here response.

When I was living in Colorado, Salida was little more than a dropping-off point for white water rafting on the Arkansas River, which skirts the north side of town. It also provided some of the

> **LUNCH @**
>
> **SMALL PLATES**
> Seaweed Salad..............
> Bacon Wrapped Gorgonzola Dates..............
> White Truffle Oil Fries, Truffle Aioli..............
> Pork Sesame Pot Stickers, Cilantro Mint Pesto..............
> Beets, Micro Greens, Pear & Gorgonzola Salad..............
> Red Wine Pickled Egg, Whole Grain Mustard, Red Onion J
> Rabbit & Antelope Cherry Habanero Sausage, w/ Cole Sl
>
> **SALADS**   11
> Asian Salad   *cucumber, wonton, sesame*

nearest (and cheapest) lodging for the Monarch Ski resort seventeen miles to the west. I quickly discovered that like much of the rest of Colorado, it has gentrified.

Having arrived before Susie and Jim, I decided to have a quick bite at what looked to be an old mountain bar. All I wanted was French fries, which I could have had, albeit with truffle oil and a hefty price. Other "small plates" included seaweed salad and rabbit/antelope sausage.

My friends were staying at the Palace Hotel, a self-described premier historical boutique inn. Surprisingly, they allowed pets, namely Jim and Susie's German Shepherd, Fifi. Noting this lenient policy would have unpleasant consequences for me a couple months later in Minnesota.

Susie and Jim's life revolved around Fifi to the point that much of our time together was spent walking the dog. I had no complaints as Salida, which means exit in Spanish but is pronounced with a long "i" instead of "saleeda," sits in an idyllic mountain-rimmed valley. There are certainly far worse places to contemplate retiring.

I was back on the road by mid-afternoon, allowing myself just enough time to get home before dark. As I retraced my steps of the previous day, I crested a hill on the brief east-west turn of US 285 north of Santa Fe just before sunset. A car had pulled over on the side of the road and a man was photographing the stunning landscape ahead. The mesas, backed by the setting sun, ranged in color from deep coral to pink to lavender to royal purple. I wished I'd done the same, but as is so often the case, I was in road-warrior mode, anxious to get home and see how the kitties were doing.

And of course, the cats were fine. Andy greeted me at the door, while Sauks crawled out from underneath the bed.

In the following days, I noticed Sauks was spending all his time under the bed, to the point where I sometimes could not lure him out with food. The latter part particularly troubled me. Sauks, like his owner, takes his food very seriously.

Sauks is also nearly ten years old. Unlike dogs, that's not quite elderly, but it is still getting up there and it was at about that stage that Murphy began to fail.

Crap, I thought, if he keeps this up I'm going to have to take him to a vet. Hiding all the time is usually the first sign a cat is ill.

Then a thought occurred to me. His carrier was still under the kitchen table. When taking either cat to the vet, I knew better than to bring one from the garage into the house. That simple act would set off a full-fledged-feline alarm, resulting in frantic searches for inaccessible-by-humans hiding places. But that carrier had been sitting there for some days, so it couldn't be an issue, could it? Just in case, I threw it back in the CRV.

Problem solved.

Sauks immediately came out from underneath the bed, begging for food.

Chapter 7: All cats stay indoors

June 29, Tijeras

If I'd had to bet which cat would figure out how to open the screen door in Tijeras, my money would have been on Sauks.

With previous cats, I'd occasionally let them out in my Houston garden, albeit under close supervision. It was often hair raising as cats are highly skilled at disappearing and never come when called, but I didn't suffer a mishap until Sammy. While that tragedy happened on Mike's watch, it just as easily could have been mine.

That's it, I thought. All cats from here on stay indoors, no matter how much they protest.

As I noted earlier, Sauks was a garage cat with outdoor privileges when I adopted him. I wondered how he would take to a strictly indoor life. The funny thing is, Sauks didn't complain for at least a year.

The first time I saw Sauks was on a bright May morning a few weeks after Jack's passing. I drove across my neighborhood to the quiet cul de sac my pet sitter lived on. Tamorra called Sauks and after a few minutes he strolled casually across the street and calmly sat in my lap while we discussed the cat transfer.

So Sauks came home with me and was perfectly happy indoors, until one day out of the blue he decided it was time to go back out. No way, I kept telling him over and over.

Sauks didn't give up and finally I caved. I'd come back from a trip to Florida with a dreadful case of the flu. Between burning up with a raging fever and Sauks's relentless meowing, I let him out in a desperate attempt for some peace and quiet. A half an hour or so later, it occurred to me that he had vanished. I found him about four doors up the street, exploring a neighbor's garage.

"That's it, buddy," I said. "Your outdoor privileges have been revoked for all time."

And I've stuck to that vow, and even though it's been at least five years since he's been outside, Sauks still goes to the back door at least once a day and demands to be let out.

What part of this don't you get, cat?

Ironically, in the confines of our tiny casita in Tijeras, Sauks seemed to have little interest in going outside. Rather it was Andy who got out into the wild.

The great escape happened while a friend from Louisiana was visiting. This friend was highly amused that I was traveling with cats and had noted, quite correctly, that Andy is spoiled rotten. But he could never remember his name and kept calling him Charley.

"Is Charley there?" he'd tease when calling from Lafayette. This always left me flummoxed as my brother's name is Charlie, but gradually I caught on. Andy? Charley? Why not have two names?

So my Cajun friend swapped the heat and humidity of the Gulf Coast to spend a few days with me in the high, dry heat of New

Mexico. One of our nights together we were sitting outside watching another incredible Sandia sunset when we heard a noise from inside.

"One of the cats," I commented lazily.

When I returned indoors to refill my glass of wine a bit later, I discovered the front door's screen had been torn loose. Sauks was sitting nearby, studying the narrow opening, no doubt gauging the slim chances of squeezing his chubby body through it. Andy, on the other hand, was AWOL.

Naturally, I went into a full gut-wrenching panic. The casita was surrounded by a thousand places for a cat to hide and plenty of wildlife. Furthermore, it was already dusk. My first hunch was to circle the house, and there was Andy, sitting beneath the bird feeder. Watching it from the bathroom window consumed most of his waking hours, and now he'd found a way to get closer.

My Louisiana friend promptly fixed the screen door with a bit of duct tape, but Andy was a quick study. He learned to bop his head against the door until he jarred the hook latch loose. Then he'd slip his slender feline figure through the few inches of space between the doors. Again probably realizing he was too chunky, Sauks never attempted to follow.

For the rest of my stay in Tijeras, I'd block the screen doors with a chair. When leaving, I'd carefully close and lock the outside doors. I shuddered to think how many times I'd left Sauks and Andy there without taking those precautions.

My status as the woman who Travels with Cats has continued since our summer tour of the center of the country. I must say Sauks and Andy have only gotten more contrary as they've become accustomed to the drill. A week before the following Thanksgiving, I grabbed the two critters and we took off for Arkansas, where I was going to help my sister Susan cook at the hunting lodge she and her husband own between Little Rock and Memphis.

My brother-in-law had declared in advance Sauks and Andy were not welcome. I could not leave them behind since I'd listed my house on Airbnb and didn't know when I'd be returning to Houston. The solution was to leave them at Susan and Jeff's mostly empty house, which was an hour's drive from the lodge. The house was being packed up in preparation for being put on the market.

I got a late start out of Houston that November morning, and it was well after dark when I arrived at their house, which sits on five wooded acres northeast of Little Rock. I pulled the car around their circular drive so the headlights illuminated the front door. Sauks and Andy were on full alert, knowing they were about to get out of the car.

I found the key, as instructed, hidden under a rock under a bucket. I can be a bit of a moron with locks and it took two turns to unlatch the huge double iron doors, which led me to suspect they'd not been locked in the first place.

Spooky, I thought, as I first let Andy and then Sauks into the dark, cavernous house. Someone a bit more nervous than me probably would have scoured every corner and closet to determine it was indeed unoccupied. Instead, I left that up to Sauks and Andy as I turned on lights and poured myself a glass of wine.

The three of us had a pleasant evening. I slept in a luxurious canopied bed that was one of the few pieces of furniture remaining. Sauks and Andy mostly roamed after being cramped in the Honda for eight hours.

The next morning, Susan requested I make a run to Walmart. I thought I'd locked those gigantic iron doors, but there was a stiff wind out of the south and upon my return I found them wide open.

"Sauks. Andy," I yelled tearing through the house. Quickly concluding they had succumbed to the call of the wild, I returned to the front door, where Sauks was standing in something of a panic. He gratefully darted indoors.

Okay, one cat accounted for. Unfortunately, it was the one with some street sense. I looked at the busy highway at the end of the drive and prayed Andy had the sense not to head in that direction.

"Andy," I screamed as I went around the left side of the house. Then acting on instinct, I circled back to the right. "Andy!" I yelled again. To my great relief, he poked his head around the corner.

By the time we met in my brother-in-law's huge patch of sweet potato vines, nipped by the previous night's frost, both of us were shaking, partly from relief, partly from fear.

Sauks and Andy spent the next three nights in that house alone while I went to the lodge. I checked that door many, many times to make sure I had indeed latched and locked it. Nonetheless, a huge wave of relief would wash over me each time I pulled in the driveway to see those doors still firmly closed.

Chapter 8: Black Cat Art

July 16: Tijeras to Abiquiu and back; 114 miles

In the two months I spent in the Sandias, I was surprised by how much I felt at home. When I'd mention in passing I was there for the summer, I was invariably asked if I had friends or family in New Mexico.

"No," I'd reply. "It's just me and my cats. But I've always liked it here."

Upon reflection, I believe one of the reasons New Mexico felt like home is because it is located between the two states where I have spent most of my adult life: Texas and Colorado. During my decade of driving up from Houston, I often thought if I didn't have ties in Colorado I wouldn't bother to go further than New Mexico.

For one thing, New Mexico is as friendly as Texas. In my two months in the Land of Enchantment, not once did someone give me shit for being from Texas. That is hardly the case in Colorado. Within the first twenty-four hours of

67

any given trip to Colorado it seems I'm on the defensive, even occasionally on the receiving end of verbal assaults from friends or family. Hey, Texas has its share of flaws (politics come to mind) but please do not call my home a shithole (I literally have had friends do so). The state is surprisingly friendly, diverse, and, after nearly thirty years, home.

As far as cities go, proximity to mountains aside, I much prefer Houston to Denver. Located at the junction of Cajun culture to the east, Deep South vibes in the Piney Woods to the north, stereotypical Texas to the west, and the muddy armpit of the Gulf of Mexico to the south, Houston is great in a funky no-one-really-wants-to-live-here way that appeals to my contrary nature. Brutal summers are offset by six to seven months of quite nice weather, at least four of which are divine. People are friendly and, thanks to a culturally diverse population, the food is so good only New Yorkers dine out more often. Over the years, I have cultivated many dear friends and happy memories on this swampy, bug-infested, flat-as-a-pancake coast.

While I frequently head to Big Bend and other West Texas destinations beyond San Antonio for that Wild West experience I constantly crave, the state simply doesn't have large mountain ranges and nearly unlimited miles of public land to explore. New Mexico provided that missing piece of the puzzle.

I had no idea how much I'd truly missed the high country until I was there. But then that was a survival technique I'd developed when I first moved to Houston. The culture and geographical shock had been overwhelming and for at least a year I was terribly homesick. But due to my job, finances, and marriage (roughly in that order) I could not go back to Colorado. Therefore, knowing if I thought about the mountains I would go mad, I simply disciplined myself not to.

I was prepared for the why-New-Mexico-rather-than-Colorado question from my friends and family just to the north. The answer was easy: closer to Texas, less expensive, less crowded. I wasn't going to insult them by pointing out that New Mexico also has a wonderful local cuisine and a more vibrant art scene.

Of all the writers and artists inspired by the intense light and multi-hued high desert landscape of New Mexico, perhaps none is more renowned than Georgia O'Keeffe. I don't recall my first awareness of O'Keeffe. Certainly, it was before I bought a Santa Fe Chamber Music Festival poster featuring her "Cliffs beyond Abiquiu" on Don and my honeymoon in 1982.

Despite having faded to a faint image in a pale pink blush, the framed print still hangs in my bedroom in Sugar Land. It bears a small scar from the time Don threw a dish at me and broke the original glass. I don't recall what I said to incite his anger, as the most innocent comment could light his fuse. I do remember it took me awhile to have it reframed as we were chronically short of money. In retrospect, my attempts at repair should have stopped with the poster rather than extend to my marriage.

I've been to the Georgia O'Keeffe museum in Santa Fe multiple times, although my first attempt failed. It was 1997 and the museum had just opened to much fanfare and praise. Don had died seven months earlier, so I was flush with a clean financial slate and his life insurance rather than just a few free dollars on a nearly maxed out credit card.

Rather than make the usual day-and-a-half-day drive from southeast Texas, I flew into Albuquerque and rented a car. My plan was to see the museum and then drive on to Denver in the same day. It wasn't hard to find the museum because the line to get in was around the block. I have no tolerance for such queues and sadly drove on.

The first time I made it indoors was with Mike a few years later when the lines had dissipated. Mike was a big O'Keeffe fan, and consequently I have two additional prints in my house that have far happier memories than the "Abiquiu Cliffs." One is her 1927 Red Poppy, which hung over Mike's bed before he moved in with me. The other is a simple print of a purple petunia Mike bought after seeing the original in San Francisco. It is one of my most treasured possessions as his gift coincided with him telling me he loved me for the first time.

Mike was somewhat disappointed at the rather limited collection in Santa Fe. O'Keeffe, unlike most artists, was a commercial success virtually all her working life, so finding pieces that weren't already in collections, private and public, proved a challenge for the museum curators. That is the reason I make a point of going whenever I'm in Santa Fe: there are a few anchor pieces but much of the rest of the exhibit rotates.

My next visit to the museum was July 16, 2009, on what would have been Mike's forty-fourth birthday. It was a bittersweet day. Mike had been gone five months and being in Santa Fe just made the pain of losing him that much sharper. But his teenaged niece was with me, and introducing her to O'Keeffe provided a nice bit of symmetry.

After leaving the museum we strolled two or three blocks to the square, where I spotted a print of a watercolor by a local artist called "Black Cat at Nite in Santa Fe NM." It was to be my memorial to the also recently departed cat, Sammy.

"Where are you from?" the woman asked while wrapping it up.

"Houston," I said.

"Do you like it?"

"Yes, I met the love of my life there," I said, sparing her any of the sad details.

As many times as I'd been to the O'Keeffe museum, I'd not seen her home in Abiquiu, largely because it requires advance booking. With nearly two full months in New Mexico, I decided it was time to rectify that and invited Robbie to go along. We left Tijeras promptly at 6:30 am in order to make the nine am tour.

Abiquiu is a tiny village in the Chama River Valley, some fifty miles northwest of Santa Fe. It took O'Keeffe ten years to acquire the property. At the time it was no more than a crumbling adobe structure owned by the Catholic church, which was loathe to let it go for one reason or another. O'Keeffe already owned Ghost Ranch another fifteen miles up the road, but she wanted this property because it had irrigation rights dating back to the Spanish and, good Wisconsin farm girl she was, she wanted a garden.

That garden was and is key to the property, still planted as to her specifications, and still irrigated every Monday with water from the Chama. The house was left pretty much the way it was when O'Keeffe died at the age of ninety-eight in 1986. I was struck by how familiar it was, much like the farm kitchen in the house I grew up in, down to the pressure cooker and mason jars for canning vegetables.

While there is a famous photo of O'Keeffe with a Siamese cat, her true loves were her chows and I took a photo of the faded "Beware of Dog" sign still hanging on her gate.

Once the tour was over, Robbie and I made our way back to Santa Fe for lunch and another look at the O'Keeffe museum. From there, in a perfect déjà vu moment we walked back to the square. I flashed back to 2009, looked across the street and thought I saw the same artist.

"Have you been at this spot long? I asked, flipping through her watercolors.

"Yes, for . . . oh I'm not sure how many years now."

"I'm pretty sure I have one of your prints from a visit in 2009."

Coming across a watercolor portrait of a black cat with his head cocked, I was now sure of it. I promptly bought it as it bears more than a passing resemblance to Andy, right down to the copper eyes with a hint of green around the irises. That was when it occurred to me it was once again July 16. It would have been Mike's fifty-first birthday.

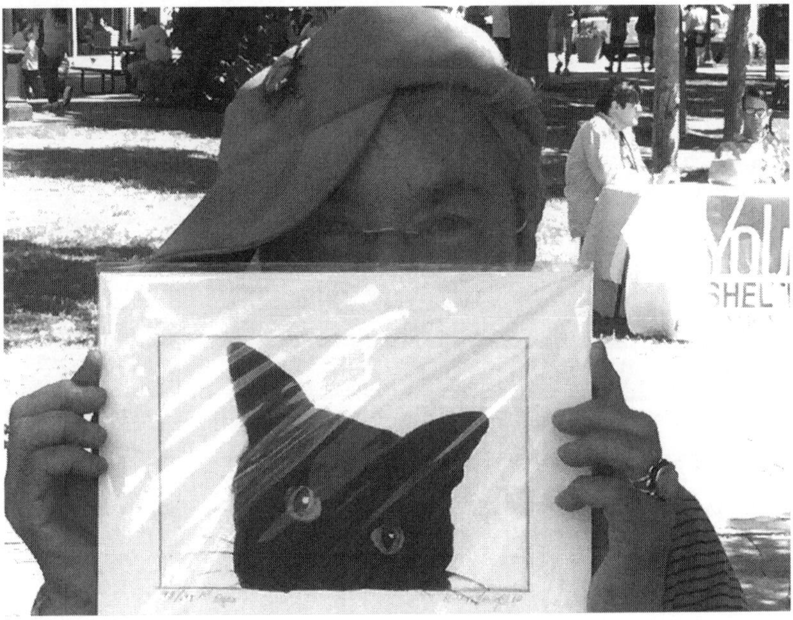

Chapter 9: Service Animals

July 19-20, Tijeras to the Grand Canyon and back; 810 miles

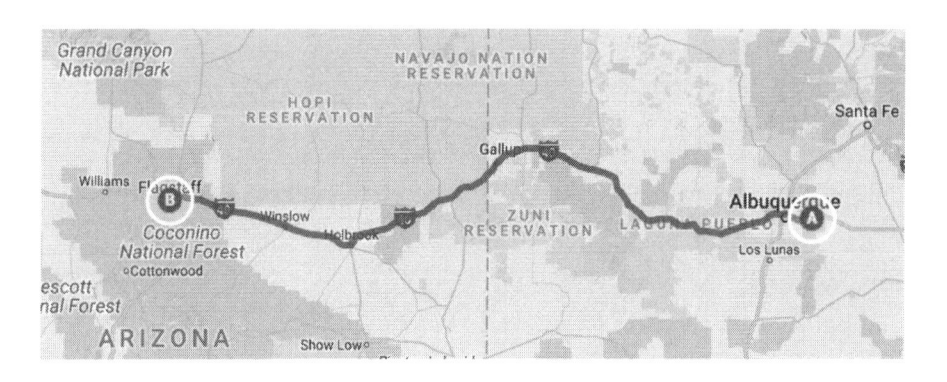

Here's a question for the ages: are cat ladies crazier than single women with tiny dogs? And while contemplating mysteries of the universe, are women living alone with animals any nuttier than single men with pets? In the latter case, we're generally talking about dogs, but I've known a few men who are devoted cat owners. My stance is we are all crazy in our own unique ways.

A friend recently complained about a girlfriend's dog who keeps interfering with their sex life, using their horizontal bodies as a hurdle. Cats are terrible little voyeurs and it is my preference to ban them from the bedroom under those circumstances. I recall Mike and I once making love when he burst out laughing.

"What?" I asked.

"Look over your shoulder."

I did, and there was Jack, just inches from my ear, watching us intently.

75

There was no bedroom door in the tiny casita I'd rented in New Mexico, which was nothing more than a one-room adobe stable that had been renovated and divided into three spaces. I was pleased to discover Sauks and Andy weren't particularly interested in anything my Louisiana friend and I did together. That said, we did get pounced on once by Andy, who found our enjoyment of each other's company no hindrance to his access to a bit of birdwatching from the window above the bed.

Back to the differences between dog owners and cat owners, I feel compelled to state that I have nothing against dogs. We had farm dogs when I was growing up, but I attribute my preference for cats to the fact that it was my interaction with kittens that gave me the warm, fuzzy feeling my mid-twentieth-century rural upbringing generally lacked. Our barn cats quickly grew old and mangy, but there was always a new litter of kittens to cuddle and love.

I don't know how I've escaped dog ownership as an adult. I've come close on several occasions. Both Don and Mike were raised in dog families and were unfamiliar with cats when they started dating me. I'll never know why neither one of them insisted we get a dog.

My brother suggested a dog as a companion when Don died. I briefly considered it. A few years later, I would have taken my neighbors' Sheltie, Tara, if they'd let me know they were giving her up.

I'd grown quite fond of Tara, encountering her frequently while outdoors, watching her antics like chasing the spray from a sprinkler. Once, I met my neighbor and Tara at the mailbox. Marilyn and I exchanged pleasantries before she walked back in her house, closing the door on a momentarily baffled Tara. The dog only missed a beat before sensing freedom and bolting up the street. By that time, Tara knew me well enough to heed my command to return.

"Thank God!" Marilyn exclaimed when I knocked on her door with the Sheltie at my side. "Chuck would have never believed that was an accident."

It seems Marilyn was not fond of the dog and in the end, she won the day. Chuck had tears in his eyes when he told me Tara had been turned over to a Sheltie rescue league. I was sad as well, but wondered if Tara would have been half as charming bouncing around my house and chasing my cats as she was in their yard.

Tara wasn't my only close call with dog ownership. After my summers in Geneva and before my 2016 escape, I once again was trapped indoors by Houston's oppressive heat and humidity. One interminable summer evening my sister called to find me in tears.

"What's wrong?" Susan asked.

I explained that out of boredom I'd just watched *One Nation under Dog*. I knew this HBO documentary, which included footage of puppy mills and unwanted dogs being euthanized, was going to be disturbing. It began with a disclaimer that warned me as much. But, hey I'm a cat person. I could take it. Or so I thought.

"I'm going to a shelter tomorrow and adopt a dog," I sobbed.

Susan, God bless her, talked me down.

"Anne, you have three cats." Fig was still with me, probably sitting on my lap at that moment, as she always watched television with me. "And you travel all the time. You cannot get a dog."

So, despite being a cat person by nature and upbringing, I have a certain fondness for dogs and my summer travels with cats included memorable meetings with friends who are devoted dog owners.

One was with Dennis and his service dog, Otto, at the Grand Canyon. I have known Dennis since we both attended the University of Nebraska in Lincoln in the mid-1970s. Susie met him in a speech class.

"I really like him," she explained. "And I know he likes me but I think he's gay. Would you join us for lunch at the student union and tell me what you think?"

I can still see Dennis walking toward us in the bright autumn sunshine.

"What part of gay don't you see?" I wanted to ask Susie.

The three of us became drinking buddies. Dennis was the first openly gay person I knew; in the 1970s, many, if not most, were still in the closet. It wasn't easy being gay back then and Dennis was a bit crazy to begin with.

Susie, Dennis, and I kept in touch as we escaped Nebraska in different directions. Then, in the mid-1980s, Dennis and my paths crossed again. I was living in Littleton, Colorado, practically in the shadow of his attorney brother's McMansion. Dennis excused himself briefly from a family Christmas to visit me down the hill. What kind of high Dennis was on that night is anyone's guess, but I'm sure some illicit chemicals were involved. He was manic and out of control, which did nothing to ease Don's annual holiday blues. It was an excruciating evening that I vowed never to repeat.

Susie also wrote Dennis off about this time for much the same reason. Unlike Susie, while sticking to my guns to not meet Dennis in person, I continued to take his calls and send him Christmas cards. That was painless enough and he seemed to appreciate it.

Fast forward thirty years and I was still more than a bit hesitant to see Dennis. When he found out I was spending the summer outside of Albuquerque, he asked me to visit him in Tucson, where he had recently moved. I think it says something about the nomadic nature of former Nebraskans that a neighboring state—even a large western one—is considered close enough for a weekend visit. I told Dennis I didn't leave my Houston steam bath to spend even two days in the southern Arizona toaster oven in mid-July. We compromised on the Grand Canyon and I once again left Sauks and Andy in Robbie's care in Tijeras and made the five-hour-plus drive to Flagstaff.

Dennis had booked a room in a somewhat dodgy motel on Route 66 that took pets, which in his case meant Otto, a black Cairn Terrier. Apparently, all it takes to secure the status of a service animal is for a medical professional to write a letter declaring that such and such a patient needs the company of this particular animal in order to not melt down. Dennis showed me his letter, which consisted of one or two sentences to that effect.

Hmmm, I wondered. Perhaps I could declare Andy or Sauks my service animal. But then where would that leave the other one? I'd revisit this idea after my painful encounter a few weeks hence with hotel staff in Minnesota.

Otto was sweet enough. Dennis had found him on the streets of Tucson, and the story was so vague on detail I wondered if he'd stolen someone else's dog.

Over the next two days, Otto accompanied us to a Route 66 diner, the Grand Canyon where we hiked a mile along the rim and had lunch at the Angel Fire Lodge, and then to an Indian restaurant back in Flagstaff that evening. Otto proved to be easy company and wore a little red service animal vest. When it comes to being on the road, there is no doubt about it: dogs are easier than cats.

The original plan was to spend three days together, but thankfully by the end of the second day Dennis declared two were enough. He had rented a car and could save money by returning to Tucson early. Also, we'd pretty much exhausted our conversation.

As both Dennis and I were unemployed or retired (take your pick), we shared a room with Otto in the Route 66 cinderblock inn. I wasn't concerned about it in the least, figuring it was little different than spending a night with a girlfriend. However, Dennis surprised me when he casually mentioned he'd never had sex with a woman. The gay men our age had tended to give it a half-hearted try back in the day, I'm assuming because being gay was still largely frowned upon.

The topic came up not because he was interested in trying (thank god) but in his curiosity about heterosexual relationships. He quizzed me endlessly about my love life, past and present. He didn't want graphic details, but rather explanations of the subtleties of attraction, courtship, and mutual affection.

"Oh, that's how it works," he'd say time and time again, adding, "I never liked being gay."

This made me sad. With the gay lifestyle just beginning to be accepted when Dennis and I were coming of age, it was still a largely rough-and-tumble world.

Perhaps that was the reason Dennis had done a 360 on his political views. Back in the 1970s, he had been, as could be expected, a raging liberal. Now the pendulum had swung far back to the right. Dennis was a connoisseur of the wildest conspiracy theories, and fell asleep each night to a podcast of some nutcase droning on and on about the sorry state of our planet and the approaching end.

The first night I tossed and turned for hours, trying in vain to ignore this claptrap while both Otto and Dennis contently snored in the next bed. The second night I asked Dennis to please plug in his ear phones.

I wonder what it is with certain people and their fondness for the-end-is-nigh line of thinking. Not very far from where we were staying, I'd listened to a boyfriend tell me how he was looking forward to the end of the world, certain we would see it in our lifetime.

"It will be a fascinating time," he said as we made our way through Monument Valley on a late 1970s' road trip to Southern California.

We had driven through one of those spectacular desert thunderstorms and found ourselves in a surreal world of candy-colored hues heightened by the recent rain and setting sun. The dope we'd been smoking all afternoon to ward off the boredom of the road only intensified the experience.

Regarding my boyfriend's vision of the imminent end, I'd been raised by a Bible-beating mother who'd been promising Christ's return for as long as I could remember. I wasn't buying it and told him so.

I believe one thing these people share, from my born-again mother to my stoner ex-boyfriend to Dennis, who has led a very tough life indeed, is a deep-seated unhappiness with the world they inhabit.

That was my final waking thought after the two Xanax I took to ward off the doom and gloom of the podcast finally kicked in the first night I shared a room with Dennis and Otto. I don't know about your world, I wanted to say, but I quite like the one I live in. While I've arguably had my share of pain, my travels have for the most part been filled with love and laughter and beauty.

Chapter 10: Seeing the light

July 31, hiking the La Luz

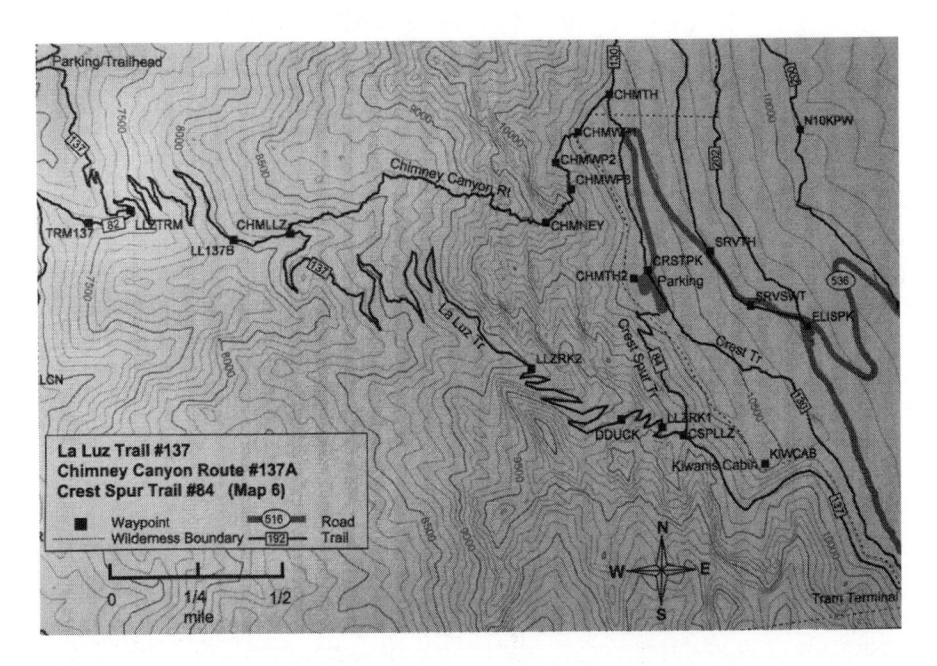

After two months of getting my "mountain legs," I was determined to hike the renowned La Luz trail, although thanks to my habit of procrastination it came down to doing it on my last day in New Mexico or not at all.

So, on Saturday, July 30, rather than pack, I got up at dawn and drove the few miles down I-40 to Tramway Boulevard, which is the major north-south route at the foot of the Sandias on the very eastern edge of Albuquerque. While the La Luz trailhead is in the northeastern portion of the city, a good ten miles north of I-40, I cruised through most of the traffic lights and still arrived early enough to snag one of the roadside spots just outside the already-full parking lot. It was not first light, but I figured it was close enough.

La Luz is on the western face of the Sandias, which I'd avoided hiking due to the scorching summer heat and general lack of shade. The far lusher East Mountains, which catch most of the monsoon rains in July and August and then the winter snows, were not only my summer home but also my personal playground, with numerous trails within short driving distance of my casita. But the climb from Albuquerque's desert floor to the top of the Sandia Crest offers stunning views of the city and the desert to the west, and I was determined to do it despite the challenge of seven miles of switch backs and 3,700 feet of elevation gain.

The origin of the name is uncertain. "The light" in Spanish, La Luz may refer to the city lights below. Another theory is that there was a mine near the top of the trail that when lit at night could be viewed from Albuquerque. The naming of the Sandia Mountains themselves is similarly fuzzy, with one camp believing the mountains looked like watermelons when the setting sun turns them red, another maintaining the Spanish mistook the wild gourds growing there as watermelons.

No matter how La Luz got its name, it is one of the most popular hikes in New Mexico, combining unsurpassed scenery with a hefty challenge all on the edge of the state's most populous city.

"Don't do La Luz," Gregory had advised. "It's too crowded."

Good advice, and thanks to my procrastination I was now doing it on a weekend. But what constitutes a crowd on a hiking trail is subjective. The first half mile of one of my favorite hikes in the Canadian Rockies, Johnston Canyon in Banff National Park, is a zoo, complete with busloads of Japanese tourists. But the climb quickly weeds out many, and once above the falls I've been so alone I worried about grizzlies.

Colorado's trails can be equally crowded, especially those close to Denver and in the Vail Valley. Shrine Ridge on Vail Pass, more than an hour's drive west of Denver, hosts hundreds on a summer weekend.

So the dozen or so people who hit the trail about the same time I did were of no concern. Rather, I was suffering from what I've come to recognize as hiking jitters. This trail is ranked as difficult and while I'm in better shape than the average person my age, I'm still nearing retirement and live most of the year at sea level. Also, I've determined that I tend to hyperventilate when ascending at higher altitudes.

Such was the case that morning. In the first ten minutes or so on the trail, I considered turning around. Was I fit enough? How long would it take? When I got to the top, how far was it to the tram? And once I came down on the tram, how long was the hike back to the trailhead?

Already huffing and puffing, I came across a man who appeared to be well into his ninth decade. He was hiking slowly but steadily with the assistance of two hiking poles. And he was wearing a vintage, brown U.S. Forest Service uniform. His exotic appearance told me he knew this trail well.

"How long will it take me to get to the top?" I asked.

"Depends. The best runners can make it in under two hours." Father Time gave me a hard, appraising look. Did my advanced years and flatlander status give me away? "For you I'd say hike until you're tired and then turn around."

"I thought I'd take the tram down and then hike back to the trailhead."

"A lot of people make that mistake. That adds another three miles with a 700-foot elevation gain and no shade." He paused to look at the sky. "Doesn't look like we'll have any cloud cover. I'd start hiking back down when I feel tired."

While far from encouraging, that sounded like good advice. Adjusting my expectations, I started the climb on long switchbacks through juniper and pinion. I had worried about heat, but the sun was still well behind the mountains above me. Some hikers passed me, I passed others. The trail runners passed all of us. Then I found myself passing groups of hikers who in turn would get ahead of me when I paused for water, only to come across them again when they rested up ahead. I was now hiking in something of a group.

I felt free and fit, paying no attention to either time or distance. La Luz climbs through four climate zones and I soon found myself among Ponderosa pines. Granite spires rose around me and with each switch-back, I came closer to the fin-shaped formation known as The Thumb.

Pausing at an overlook, I noted young hikers checking their Garmins.

"How far have we gone?" I asked.

"Nearly five miles."

Well, if I was that close to the top there certainly wasn't any reason to turn back now. Although if I had been looking for one, the nineteen switchbacks ahead of me that crossed mammoth rockslides certainly would have qualified. It took steady balance to traverse the rocks and I was a bit shaky from the climb. It didn't help that I'd slipped and nearly fallen on the first slide. I equate this to taking a bad fall on the first ski trip or nearly losing control of the car in the first snowstorm of the year; it puts you at a psychological disadvantage that haunts you the rest of the season.

Perhaps looking like I needed reassurance, some hikers who'd paused mid-way through a rockslide for refreshment told me I was doing well. It worked, providing me with a much-needed boost of confidence.

At the fork at the top of the trail, I paused. Right or left. Left promised a further half-mile climb the opposite direction from the tram. I opted for the right.

The path was narrow but flat and I was moving along steadily until I noticed that the heavy woods to my left were disguising what was essentially a sheer drop off. I was on a catwalk hundreds if not thousands of feet up. My knees went weak. Once descending Tree Spring, a careless stumble resulted in bone-jarring fall. Stunned, I had picked myself up, dusted off, and slowed down. It served as a reminder that I was tired and no longer terribly steady.

Now in a similar state, such a mishap would be a disaster. I would fly off the cliff and no one would ever know what had happened to me. Such a realization did little for my state of mind. That last mile was interminable.

Finally, I heard and then saw the tram. I had planned a celebratory lunch at the High Finance restaurant, where I'd eaten on so many Tree Spring hikes the wait staff knew me. But now I just wanted off that mountain. I got on the first car down and ate at the Mexican restaurant at the foot of the tram. I don't know if the cheese enchiladas I ordered were indeed the best I'd ever had, or it was just the effect of extreme hunger.

I was still three miles from my car. I'd chatted with numerous hikers on the trail. Some had friends driving around the backside of the mountain to pick them up at the crest. Others had someone meeting them at the bottom of the tram.

"Uber," one hiker told me.

Hmmm, that sounded like a plan. So, while waiting for my food I downloaded the app. I hit "pick me up" while paying the bill.

My driver, a man about my age, was waiting outside.

"Where to?" he asked.

"The La Luz Trailhead. Do you know where it is?"

"I make this run all weekend long."

It turned out he was a fellow Texan who'd moved to Albuquerque from Austin when that city banned Uber.

There were more than a few cars still at the trailhead, so I wasn't the last one down. But then others were probably making the return trip on foot. I drove back to my casita in Tijeras thrilled with my achievement but exhausted. With Sauks and Andy stretched out in the afternoon sun, I made some minor attempts at packing, knowing I'd really have to hustle in the morning if I was going make it to a six o'clock dinner the next night in Denver.

Part 3: Leaving the West

Chapter 11: The adventure begins

July 31: Tijeras to Littleton, Colorado, by way of Golden:
Nearly 500 miles

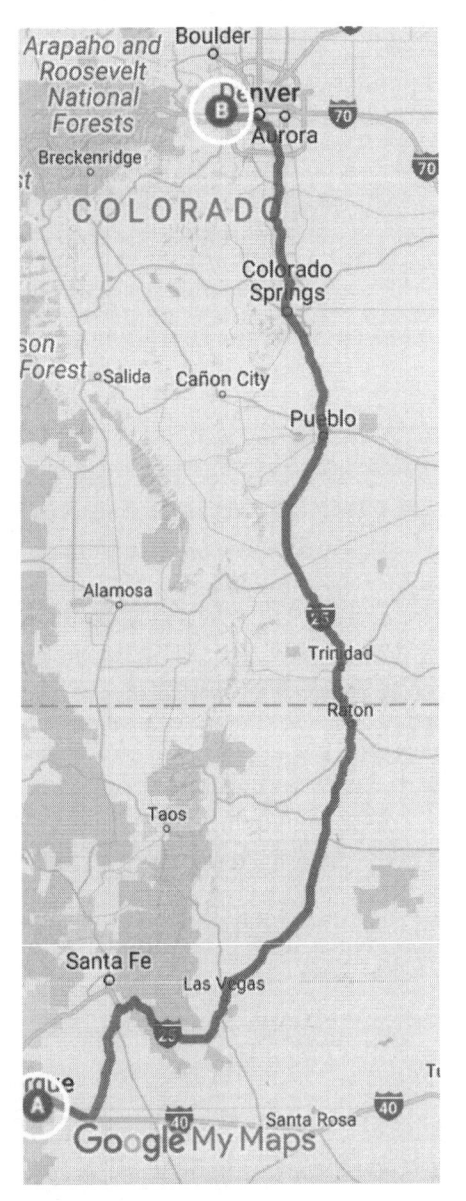

On the last day of July, Sauks, Andy, and I hit the road for what was to be a five-week trip catching up with friends and family across several states. Since all of them lived in much nicer places than summertime Houston (but then what isn't nicer than that), it was something I'd dreamed of doing once I was retired. Now it was time to put it to the test.

Leaving Tijeras was sad although I'd already decided to return the following summer. My La Luz hike the previous day had left me little time or energy for packing, so it took much of the morning to gather my belongings. This in turn provided Sauks and Andy plenty of time to fret and anticipate another toss in the car. Fortunately, our cramped casita had few hiding places. With minimum struggle, I shoved both in the car and we were off.

My first destination was Susie's in Littleton, a southern suburb of Denver probably most renowned for the April 1999 Columbine High School massacre in which twelve students and a teacher were killed. It is best accessed by I-25, so it was with some sadness that after taking the Turquoise Trail northward to Santa Fe, I made a right-hand turn onto the interstate, rather than proceeding into Colorado on the mountain route of US 285. Not only is I-25 not nearly so scenic, but it is rife with memories of my earlier life in the west, many of which are heartrending.

At least the first sixty-five miles from Santa Fe to Las Vegas (yes, there is another Las Vegas outside of Nevada), is pretty. Here I-25 becomes an anomaly among U.S. interstate highways in that it reverses course, taking a southward route to traverse the heavily forested mesas that mark the southern edge of the Sangre de Cristo Mountains.

It was in this stunning landscape, somewhere between Glorieta and Pecos, that I camped on an early trip to New Mexico. It was a Memorial Day Weekend in either 1979 or 1980 and my sister Marcia, our friend Nora, and I decided it was high time we visit the neighboring state to the south. Too short on funds to afford a hotel room in pricey Santa Fe, we retreated to a make-shift campsite off a dirt road in the Santa Fe National Forest after a day of sightseeing among the adobe buildings that are among the oldest in America and vast array of shops featuring the works of local artisans.

We felt very bold indeed camping along the Pecos River without any men (I've since taken it a step further and now camp alone), although we were a bit spooked when some locals stopped by at dusk to ask if we'd seen their dog, adding casually they'd lost it when the canine took off after a bear. Hard to say whether this was true or just thrown in as a joke.

That night I dreamed I was attacked by a bear only to wake up flailing. Something heavy and indeed alive was on top of me. Fortunately, rather than a bear it was Nora. She and Marcia had set up air mattresses while I was sleeping on the ground. We were on a bit of a slope so during the night Nora had slid off her perch and onto me.

This is a stretch of I-25 in northern New Mexico I'd also traveled many times with Don. On our honeymoon in Santa Fe, we somehow came up with the idea of driving out of town for dinner at the Lamy Legal Tender. If I were to guess why it was because it required driving rather than walking and was away from the crowds of tourists, as both walking and crowds were despised by Don. No matter the reason, it became a tradition and we repeated the trip several times during later anniversary trips.

The historic town of Lamy was originally the drop-off point for people traveling to Santa Fe by train, as it was the end of the rail line due to the same difficult geography that dictates I-25 heads the opposite direction for several dozen miles. This was the initial point of arrival for many of the Dream Team Robert Oppenheimer hired to assist him the Manhattan Project. They got off the train at Lamy and made their way northward to Los Alamos by car to develop the atomic bomb that ended World War II.

The Legal Tender was housed in a saloon built in the 1880s, providing a colorful evening away from the Santa Fe tourists. A Google search reveals it closed in 2013 and is reputedly haunted; perhaps it is one of the spots Don's spirit visits as we did have a good time there. I like to think he haunts the places where we were happy.

At Las Vegas, I-25 finally turns north for the run into Colorado on a classic front range drive: the Rocky Mountains to the west and the Great Plains to the east, or left and right if you're heading north as I was.

I exited at Wagon Mound, New Mexico, to rearrange the huge pile of stuff in the back of the CRV that was blocking my vision. Raising the hatch alerted both Sauks and Andy, who had been sprung from their carriers just a few miles up the Turquoise Trail. Then a few miles later, I had to pull over again for an OCD check to make sure both cats were still in the car.

The original plan was to meet Susie and Jim at their house and then ride with them across Denver to join a friend in Golden for dinner. Those plans evaporated when I hit stop-and-go-traffic north of Colorado Springs.

Driving into Colorado from New Mexico, I was immediately struck by the increase in traffic. A month earlier, my nephew had refused to swing back through New Mexico after his vacation in Wyoming. He opted for the far-less scenic route back to Arkansas through Kansas just to avoid I-25 traffic through Colorado. When I moved to Colorado in the late 1970s, people were already talking about an urban corridor stretching all the way from the Springs to Fort Collins and each time I go back, that prediction seems closer to realization.

So it wasn't a big surprise when somewhere between Monument and Larkspur, traffic on I-25 ground to a halt.

Great, I thought as I inched forward, it is Sunday afternoon and I'm in a traffic jam of weekenders heading back to Denver. Even in the 1980s I'd experienced this phenomenon coming into town on I-70 from mountain outings. That was one of reasons Don and I chose US 285 to the southwest as our escape route into the high country.

I called Susie to tell her I was going to be late, and she suggested I meet them in Golden instead.

"It's cloudy here," she said, "and in the low eighties. Your cats should be fine in the car."

Used to Houston's summers that heat a car into a danger zone within minutes and the searing sun of Albuquerque's desert floor, I'd already determined Colorado's day of light clouds was going to present no danger to Sauks and Andy.

An hour or two later I pulled up to a restaurant in a new strip center. It was now completely overcast and the deeply shadowed foothills loomed high over me. Perhaps most famous for being the home of Coors Brewery, Golden long ago spilled from its historic center in the foothills to form a sprawling suburb on the very western edge of Denver.

While I'd worked in an office park in this part of Golden for a few months in 1981, Golden has grown so much nothing looked familiar. I poured a bit of water into a bowl for the cats, which they ignored. It would be the first of many times they'd be left in the car while I was en route from Point A to Point B, but they pretty much stayed in hibernation mode until freed into a place without wheels.

"Fifi's sick," were practically Susie's first words when I found their table.

It seems Fifi, their eleven-year-old German Shepherd, had collapsed while they were hiking earlier that weekend. I could see the anguish on Susie's face and knew all too well the gnawing sense of dread she was feeling.

"She's better now," Susie continued, "but we're taking her to the vet first thing in the morning."

After dinner, we headed back to Susie and Jim's. They had an errand to run, so I got there first. I shoved Andy and Sauks back into their carriers so the three of us could sit on the front stoop. I listened to the crickets in the dark, but inside the house Fifi only let out a few modest barks. This deepened my concern.

On a visit a year earlier, I'd arrived after ten and Fifi greeted me with a cacophony of deep-throated woofs. Just a few weeks earlier when I'd approached Susie and Jim in Salida, the German Shepherd had also gone into full-protection mode. She took her guardianship of Susie and Jim very seriously, but now it seemed she could barely summon the energy.

When Susie and Jim arrived, I hustled Sauks and Andy into the guest bedroom. It would be the first of many transports from the car to lodging in the next few weeks.

Chapter 12: Princess Fifi (April 29, 2005-August 1, 2016)

August 1, Littleton, Colorado

The prognosis on Fifi was swift and brutal. She had cancerous tumors and internal bleeding. It was untreatable. There was no hope and she was in pain. The vet would be making a house call at six that evening to put her down.

Fifi's dog bed was dragged to the patio door in the kitchen, and Susie, Jim, and I gathered for one of those heartrending, waiting-for-the-end days of suspended animation.

How many times had I been through this in just the last decade? Every time I thought it could not get any more heartbreaking, somehow it did. But this was my first time saying goodbye to a dog, albeit not mine.

Fifi, who had been so full of life just a few weeks earlier when she joined us in Salida, seemed to fade as the day progressed. We took turns sitting on the floor petting and reassuring her in low voices.

I tried to be philosophical, which is easy only if the pet isn't yours. Fifi was eleven years old, which is elderly for a large dog. She was deeply loved and had enjoyed a good, active life right up until the end. Jim and Susie, bless them, listened to my lame musings without throwing anything at me or telling me to shut up. I'm sure I annoyed the hell out of them, but they were kind enough to focus on Fifi instead.

As a cat owner, it was rewarding to have an animal respond to our ministrations. Fifi truly appreciated our company. And, not only Susie and Jim's. She gratefully received the little bit of comfort I offered her, returning my reassuring pets with a sad, panting smile. It was beyond tragic to know this lovely creature was suffering and only had hours left.

When cats are ill their instinct is to hide. No matter how much they cuddled with you when they were alive and well, when it comes to the end they want to suffer and die alone, a hard lesson I learned during my childhood on the farm where we had many barn cats.

I knew Murphy was seriously ill when she spent an entire weekend soaking up the sun under the crepe myrtle tree in the garden, refusing to eat or drink and shrugging off my efforts to offer aid. Shortly after I lost her, I lucked upon a bit of cat art at the local garden center that is a spitting image of her. It sits under that crepe myrtle tree, where Murphy is buried.

Recently, while running in my neighborhood I came across a couple carrying a disoriented cat.

"I guess she's ready to check out," they told me.

The thin, brown tabby was clinging to the woman's shirt, her eyes glassy and blank.

"She's very old and disappeared yesterday. We just found her."

The cat looked a great deal like a garage cat I had that lived to be nearly twenty. I didn't like having an outdoor cat, but she never strayed further than the neighbors' yards on either side of me and certainly never crossed the street. However, in the end she wandered off to die alone. After a few hours of frantic searching, a neighbor looked at the photo I was clasping and said: I just saw that cat. He pointed me in the right direction and I found her some blocks away,

101

sitting dazedly in a stranger's yard. It was as if she didn't want to inconvenience me by dying at home.

So, being able to sit vigil with an ailing dog who appreciated my presence was a new experience, albeit it one that was heartbreaking.

I've known Susie to love many a dog, but never one as much as she loved Fifi. In turn, Fifi was very protective and would ward off anyone approaching with ferocious barking. Fifi had greeted me in Salida with a series of ear-splitting barks. I stopped a few feet away and spoke to her in a low, reassuring voice until she calmed down. As Susie, a fellow Nebraskan correctly noted, this was a skill I'd learned as a child on the farm when dealing with neighbors' aggressive dogs. But then Susie loved me, so Fifi loved me in turn.

First impressions aside, Fifi had a very tender soul, which was the reason her extraordinary life was not the one initially intended for her. Born in late April 2005 and christened Fiona, she had been bred to detect bombs in Afghanistan. However, by the time she was six months old it became apparent to her trainers that she was not aggressive enough for the task. Consequently, Fifi was given to the Colorado Springs police department. However, it seemed she was too sweet tempered for law enforcement as well and she ended up in a kennel.

As is often the case in life, these setbacks proved a blessing in the end as Fifi consequently found the first great love of her life. Ed, a retired policeman, adopted her at the age of two. The two of them lived together happily for three years in the Willow Creek neighborhood of Littleton.

It was in a Willow Creek park in the fall of 2009 that Susie met Fifi. She was working as a pet sitter when Ed struck up a conversation with her.

"Are you a dog walker?" he asked.

When she said yes, he asked if she would walk Fiona. So, Susie took Fiona out once a week from November through the spring of 2010. Then Fifi's life took another tragic turn, when Ed had surgery for a brain tumor that turned out to be malignant. Since Ed was very ill, Susie started walking Fiona daily. The former policeman went downhill quickly and when he was hospitalized later in the summer, Fiona stayed with Susie and Jim. Susie took the dog to visit Ed in the hospital.

"It was really special to see them connect in the hospital," Susie said. "At that point, he was so sick he couldn't remember how to pet Fiona. Helping him pet her was one of the most special and bittersweet moments of my life."

Knowing the end was near, Ed asked his sister Jan to adopt Fiona. She told him she would, although her cat and townhouse's lack of outdoor space made it impossible. So, Susie took up the challenge of finding Fifi a home. Her first attempt wasn't successful, foiled by yet-another cat who had first ownership rights.

I'd venture another factor it was because Fifi wasn't going to be happy unless she had Susie and Susie's connection to Ed. So, in the end Susie and Jim adopted Fifi, despite already having two large dogs. This proved to be a bit of a challenge as they had to train her to share Susie with Zamboni and Hudson.

In the coming years, Susie and Jim lost both Zamboni and Hudson, one to illness the other to old age. Consequently, Fiona became the focus of their lives; they began to call her Princess Fifi.

I know from experience that a personal loss—be it a human or a pet—will intensify your bond with the survivor. So, I understood why Susie loved this dog more than any other and why her grief was so profound.

Just a few weeks after returning from my father's funeral, my Siamese cat, Truman, died. With those events so closely juxtaposed, I could compare the pain. Both losses were devastating, yet utterly different. That was when I realized that one of the reasons it hurts so much when your pet dies is you go through it alone. You can't count on even your closest friends and family to fully comprehend let alone share your grief.

Sharing is key. When a human being passes away, any number of people are mourning the same loss, maybe not to your extent, but they feel it nonetheless. This is not the case with animals; the heavy burden of the pain settles on your shoulders alone. If you're lucky, you have someone in your life to share the grief, but since animals (both cats and dogs) tend to choose a favorite, chances are one person will be more affected than the other. A case in point was Murphy. Mike was sad, but I was devastated. She and I had weathered Don's terrible demise together. I couldn't imagine going on without her.

Since we all knew it was Fifi's last day, Ed's sister was notified. Jan arrived mid-afternoon and then there were four of us, speaking in hushed tones, waiting for the end.

Fifi was the last living, breathing connection between Jan and her brother. She was mourning not only the dog, but once again Ed. I went through this with Jack, prolonging his life a bit too long in order to hold on to the last warm, breathing remnant of Mike.

Again, I think I said something lame like, "Fifi will soon be back with Ed." My intentions were good and hopefully not too annoying. I was drawing on the experience of being comforted when an aunt said I'd lost Jack because he wanted to be with Mike.

I'd decided early in the day to flee before the vet showed up on the premise that my presence would not be helpful. Having dealt with the death of more than a few loved ones, I was going to pass on this scene. Fortunately, a cousin across town was free for dinner, so

I was getting ready to leave the mourners to themselves when the doorbell rang. Damn. Not quite quick enough.

At the sound of the chime, Susie, who had been stoic the entire day, let out a heartrending cry that sent shivers down my spine. All day she'd shared stories about Fifi. A playful dog, Fifi was the most loyal animal they'd ever owned, content to simply sit and guard them for hours on end. She was also dainty and ladylike, rarely passing gas (long ago I'd had a roommate with a German Shepherd who could wake up the entire house with her farts), always clean, riding in the car like a human, never deigning to hang her head out the window like other dogs.

Now Susie's façade crumbled, knowing there were only minutes left before Fifi would be gone forever.

I'd cried so hard and so long after having Jack put down, the vet wondered if she should call someone to come and pick me up. And, as I've mentioned, I was such an emotional wreck after Fig was put out of her misery I was allowed to simply walk out rather than go through the motions of paying the bill. In other words, I've been there and done that more than once.

In one of those eerie coincidences, I knew Susie and Jim's vet. It had clicked some years earlier when Susie told me how Doctor Sarah had taken care of their Golden Retriever Hudson in his final days.

"Doctor Sarah?" I asked. "What's her last name?"

Yes, it was the same Doctor Sarah I'd had back in the 1980s when I was living in Littleton. I remembered her well. I'd found her when looking for a vet for Truman and Arthur, the cats that died, respectively, just after my father and just before Don. A recent-graduate, she had a brand-new practice in a recently built strip mall not too far from my home in the southern suburbs of Denver. The idea of a woman vet appealed to me and she was not a disappointment. Perhaps because she had yet to build up a clientele, Doctor Sarah took the time to sit and talk to me until my cats approached her. Since then I've had many kind vets (unlike physicians for humans, this tends to be the rule rather than the exception), but never another who took this patient an approach.

Now Doctor Sarah was intent upon the unpleasant but necessary task at hand. She'd arrived with the necessary medical paraphernalia as well as an assistant. Nonetheless, she politely listened to my recollection of our meeting decades earlier.

"When I moved to Houston I tried in vain to find a woman vet," I explained.

"Ah yes," she said. "Not easy to do in the macho world of Texas A&M."

In all my time in Texas, it has just been in the last few years I've encountered a handful of female veterinarians, all young, fairly recent graduates, including the emergency room vet who, after putting Jack down, asked if she could call a cab to take me home.

After a few minutes of awkward chit chat that was par for the day, I left Jim and Susie's in a cowardly, tail-between-my-legs rush before Doctor Sarah and her assistant could address the unpleasant business at hand.

Fifi was never far from my mind as I spent the evening with my cousin, who had warned me in advance she was not on speaking terms with her husband. The day became even more surreal when he appeared, approaching Charlene and me as we drank wine in her garden. Dan took a chair and cordially conversed with me on a number of subjects. He then retreated to the house and Charlene and I resumed our conversation. Throughout the whole episode, neither husband nor wife acknowledged the other's presence.

Sometime after the mile-high twilight had faded, I returned to my friends' quiet, dark house. Susie and Jim had already gone to bed. The house was deadly silent and memories of Fifi's protective barks haunted me. I crawled in my own bed with Sauks and Andy, who seemed to sense the pall of death and thankfully snuggled close by my side.

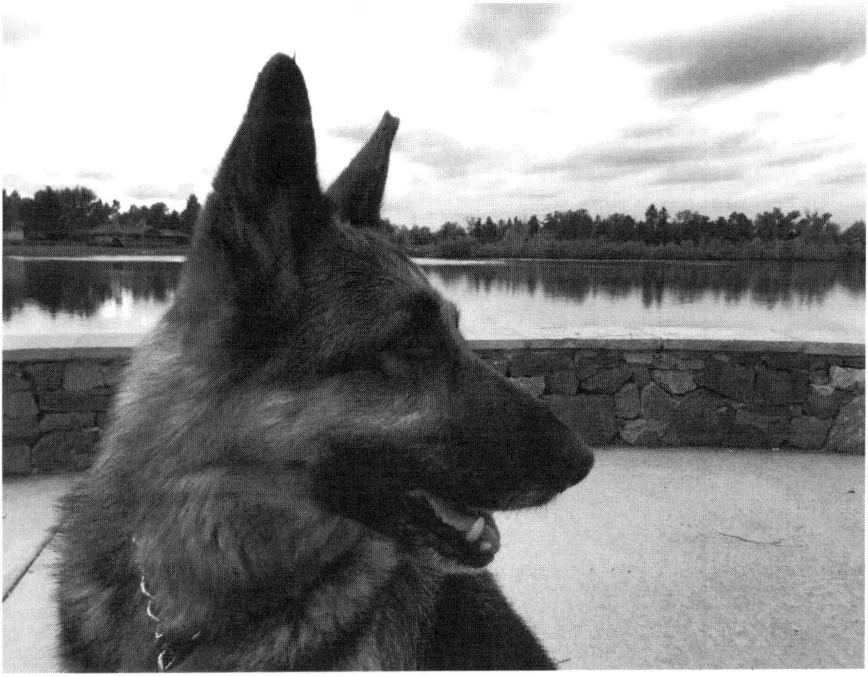

Chapter 13: Sauks's faux paw

August 2 and 3: Littleton to Berthoud and back; 110 miles

"Sauks hasn't moved all day."

I was visiting friends in Berthoud, when this text came through from Susie with the accompanying photo.

Susie was amused rather than alarmed. Despite her preference for dogs, she'd owned and understood cats and their ability to morph into virtual pieces of furniture.

With Fifi no longer a threat to Sauks and Andy, Susie had decreed they could be released from their confines in the guest bedroom. Sauks promptly took up residence on Fifi's now-vacant dog bed, which Susie found comforting. Meanwhile, Andy went exploring.

I was happy to have a place to leave the cats while catching up with friends an hour's drive to the north.

In my early years in Houston I would pack as many friends as possible into my short Colorado stays. I gave this up early on when I realized that I was not only exhausting myself but managing to piss a lot of them off in the process. They had a point: why show up on their doorstep if I only had forty-five minutes or an hour before I had to scurry off to meet someone else.

Over the ensuing years, I've selectively picked who I could fit in, trying to even it out and stay in touch with as many as possible. So, on the third day of August, in the sad aftermath of Fifi's departure, I limited it to a lunch with my New Mexico camping pal Nora, whom I'd not seen in decades and then an afternoon with friends who lived some fifty miles up the front range. Then, I'd return to Susie and Jim's that evening.

When Susie and Jim had arrived a couple nights earlier

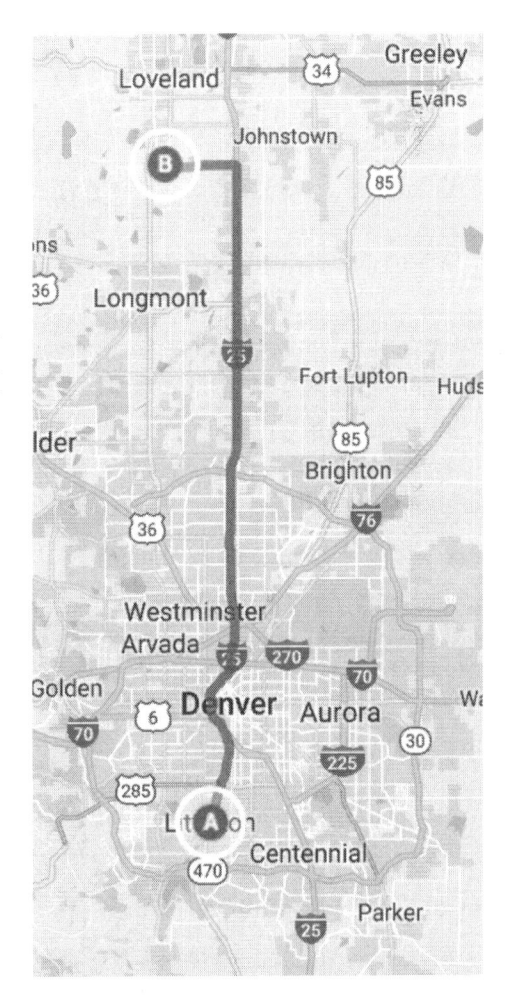

to find Sauks, Andy, and me sitting on their front steps, she had apologized for sequestering them in the guest room.

"I just don't trust Fifi. I'm not sure what she'd do with a cat."

No explanations were necessary. Fifi was a German Shepherd, bred to tear small furry animals apart. Furthermore, we were imposing upon them.

On the latter point, I am fully aware what a pain cats can be. Recently I met a friend in Tulsa who asked when he opened the door: what, no cats?

"That's just what you want," I said, "me to show up with two cats and a litter box."

I may be a cat lady, but I'm not oblivious to how weird and imposing it can get.

So what are the drawbacks of traveling with cats? The top three on my list are: one, their inherent aversion to travel, which makes it a challenge getting them in the car and then can result in persistent meowing that can literally last the entire trip; two, the reluctance of hotels to let them on their premises; and three, cats' tendency to be lousy houseguests, particularly if there are other pets on the premises.

Oddly, among the people I'd be visiting in the coming weeks, cat owners outweighed dog owners, which presented a special set of problems. Sauks and Andy can be oblivious to dogs, but some cats just will not do (and vice versa).

At Susie's, Sauks and Andy had been for the most part content in the guest bedroom. The arrival of Doctor Sarah had sent bad vibes all the way to the back of the house and they cowered behind their closed door as cats seem to have eerie extrasensory skills.

But their new quarters really weren't all that much smaller than our casita. Susie and Jim slept in the basement to accommodate their dogs, so we were the beneficiary of big windows open to the glory that is Denver in the summertime. And no one appreciates an open window more than a cat.

Which isn't to say the cats weren't happy to be set free. Sauks promptly found Fifi's huge dog bed, which was now sadly vacant and back in its traditional spot at the top of the basement steps.

"Looks good to me," he must have thought, because he settled in for a nap. That had been first thing in the morning. Now it was late afternoon and, according to Susie's text, he had yet to move.

"We've not seen Andy for a while," was her second text.

Andy and Sauks had been happier in the casita than I would have guessed. Occasionally they would surprise me by finding a new nook or cranny in our tiny space.

During the first week, Andy jumped behind the stackable washer and dryer from the bathroom vanity. Once there, he discovered the only way out was the way he'd gone in. In other words, he'd have to jump three feet up back onto the sink and he had no room to position himself for the leap.

"You're on your own, buddy," I told him. Once Andy realized I couldn't help him, it didn't take him long to get up the nerve to complete the maneuver successfully.

Now as the younger and more restless of the two cats, Andy was taking full advantage of Susie and Jim's house, which offered two floors, multiple rooms, windows in all directions, and a lovely flight of basement stairs to explore. What fun! I just hoped he was expending his excess energy in the basement rather than in Jim and Susie's living room, which is decked out with elegant mid-century furnishings.

I made it back to Susie and Jim's in time for dinner.

"Thank you, Anne. They have been such a comfort. A blessing really, to have four-legged, furry animals around."

My cats are reasonably social, on the feline scale anyway, but I was still surprised they could provide this service. I thought about venturing that when Jim and Susie were ready to get another dog, they might consider a cat as well, but let it go. I know enough not to try to sway dedicated dog people to the dark side.

We gathered in the kitchen for dinner and wine, watching the sun drop behind the Rockies. Stories of lost pets were traded as we alternated between laughter and tears. Another bottle of wine was opened. Our private wake was going well until Sauks decided it was finally time to get up. He stretched, came over to rub our legs and solicit a few pets. I reached down and scratched his head, but we were so engrossed in conversation, that no one noticed him strolling into the living room, where he promptly sunk his claws into the brand-new, cinnamon-colored sofa.

The sound of claws on leather was like nails on a chalkboard. The three of us simultaneously threw down our napkins, pushed back our chairs, and ran toward the disaster. Sauks turned as if to say, what's the big deal? I could see where he had sunk his claws into one arm of the sofa. I was mortified. Jim was furious. Susie tried valiantly to be the voice of reason. I promptly scooped up Sauks and threw him in the guestroom. Then I excused myself from the tempest in the living room to search out Andy just in case he decided to follow suit.

"It's just a tiny scratch," Susie told Jim.

He was not to be dissuaded. Proof positive that cats are evil. I apologized profusely before slinking off to bed.

Chapter 14: A drug deal

August 4: Littleton to North Denver; 19 miles

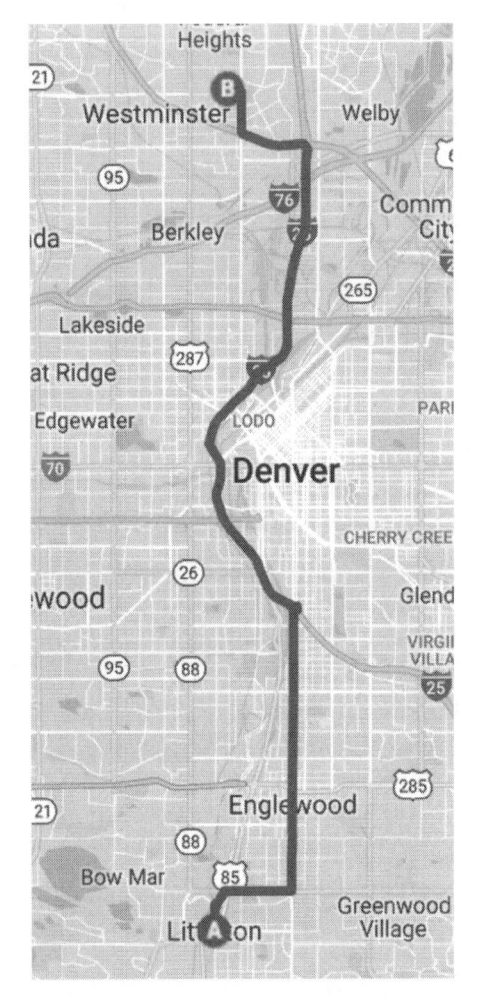

Since Sauks had worn out our welcome in one fell swoop of his paw, my plans to move on the next day proved most timely.

The second leg of my journey would take me hundred miles to Edwards in the Vail Valley to spend two nights with my sister, Marcia. But first I needed to run a couple of errands in the Denver area.

My first mission was to buy some dope. While marijuana is now legal in Colorado, I didn't know what dispensaries would be available in Vail as they are still subject to local ordinances. Also neither my sister nor brother-in-law indulge, so it seemed unfair to ask or otherwise involve them.

"There's a whole row of shops on South Broadway," Susie told me.

South Broadway was on my way to my aunt's, and having lunch with her was my second objective. Ironically, the marijuana dispensaries were in the part of town where she worked long ago when Montgomery Wards had an office there.

Now it's a row of so-so shops with the occasional funky restaurant possibly worth a stop thrown in. Sure enough there one solid block of pot shops. I drove around the block and determined there was also no shade, which was something of a concern as the cats were with me.

I cracked the windows, fed the meter, and told them, like they'd understand, I'll be back shortly.

Buying marijuana legally is an interesting experience, but I'd learned the ropes in Salida a few weeks earlier. The door to the shop I chose was locked and I was buzzed in. The front rooms of dispensaries have a wide display of wares, but they are just for show. After checking the date on your license to make sure it's still valid, you are shown to the back where the real purchases—all cash of course—take place.

As I said, friends had let me in on the drill. Sativa is good, hybrids can be nice, ask for something that won't put you under (Indica will do so—after all this is nearly medical-grade dope). I'd already determined pre-rolled joints with a filter were to my liking.

Generally, the staff tends to be attractive, professional women. This shop was the exception as I was waited on by a young man who was the epitome of a stoner.

"Let me get you some of our best stuff," he said, grabbing a huge, clear plastic bag behind the counter. Pre-rolled joints come in nice little plastic cylinders and he began rifling through them, tossing many aside on the floor.

"There's going to be hell to pay," he promised. "Whoever worked last night threw all of these in together."

While he was sorting and swearing, I had a chance to surreptitiously check out my fellow clientele. It was slow this mid-week morning, but there was a man in a suit who looked to be in his fifties, plus a few other well-dressed folks. Everyone was well past their twenties if not thirties.

I walked out with six joints, thinking that should be enough party favors for people down the road. From there it was a quick drive up the Valley Highway, as I-25 was known in its early days, to north Denver, where my aunt has lived in the same house since 1959.

Ah, the memories in this modest, one-car-garage brick ranch home. The first time our family visited from northeastern Nebraska, my maternal grandparents were with us. That must have been the summer of 1961 since Grandpa died in June of 1962. For one reason or another we didn't have directions. Having spent the eight years of my life to date on a farm with an occasional trip to the tiny towns nearby, I offered the extremely unhelpful advice that we take out the photo we had of the house and drive around until we spotted it. I have no idea why I remember this detail, except maybe because after a day or two in the big city I realized how confined my world had been so far.

And so, the years came and went with this house often at the center of both my childhood and adulthood. Mom and Dad took us to visit many times when we were kids just wanting to escape into the mountains. And then we were in high school, when we often brought along friends because we couldn't stand our siblings. One year I was so enamored with my high school boyfriend that the mountains provided little solace and I sulked the entire time.

During my college years, my friends and I often infringed upon my aunt—by then divorced—when making our way to and from football games up the road in Boulder.

After graduation, I moved to Denver where I stayed with my aunt for two weeks. She told me in advance that was all the time she was giving me to find a job and a place to live. If I couldn't achieve those goals in that time, it was back to Nebraska for me.

I'll always owe her for that tough love. Neither the job nor the apartment I found were anything to write home about, but by god I'd managed to secure both and the cornfields were behind me forever.

My aunt's house was a frequent gathering spot during the dozen years after college that I lived in the Denver area. I brought along at least two boyfriends on these visits, one of whom was Don. It was a go-to place for holiday dinners, summer barbecues, and everything in between.

The cousin I'd visited three nights earlier grew up here. One of the first batch of photos of this house we received back in Nebraska included her as a newborn in her crib. She has an older brother who was an honest-to-god hippie (as opposed to a wanna be), who lived in San Francisco's Haight-Ashbury for a while. Before that stint, he was the aloof, good-looking older cousin, disdainful of our country ways. He married while still in his teens and showed up once with a pretty young wife and an even prettier baby. Then we didn't see him again for a very long time.

During my years in Denver, this cousin again made an appearance. He was back in the Colorado mountains and had a rather personable girlfriend. Unfortunately, like his marriage, it didn't last.

After I moved to Houston, he lost his job and apartment, in that order, and was now living in his mother's basement. Never social to begin with, he isn't inclined to surface for out-of-town family, so I was surprised when I heard his footsteps on the stairs.

"Anne. Did you buy some pot while you were here?"

I looked at my aunt. Hmmm. How to answer that one. Well, it is legal right?

"Yes. In fact, I just came from there."

"Can I have some?"

Well, now I knew why I was being honored with his presence. "Yeah, I guess so." Seems I was going to be exploring the pot shops of Eagle County after all.

I went back out to the car and swatted the kitties aside as I looked through my stash. I picked the one with the goofiest name, Purple People Eater or some such thing, having no idea what I might be giving up.

"You pay her for that," my aunt demanded as I handed it over.

"How much?" he asked.

"Fifteen and let's call it even." Okay, so I added a surcharge.

He went back down to the basement. I looked at my aunt with some embarrassment. She rolled her eyes, but otherwise seemed cool.

"You have change for a twenty?" he asked when he returned.

While my aunt reached for her purse, I decided to try and make the whole situation as politically correct as possible.

"I suppose it relieves the pain in your back, right?"

The years have not been kind to my cousin. Having suffered an injury while working construction, he's hunched over and shuffles along like a man much older than his sixty-five years.

"Nah," he said, forking over three fives. "I just like to get high."

Well, so much for trying to put a good spin on it, but I had gotten my aunt's attention.

"Share that with me," she instructed him. "It might help my arthritis."

Is this woman really my mother's sister? It wasn't the first nor will it be the last time I've wondered.

Chapter 15: Sauks discovers automatic windows

August 4: North Denver to Westminster to Edwards; 118 miles

I was able to leave the cats in the car while lunching with my aunt at the Westminster Chili's. By August there is usually a hint of the upcoming fall in the air on the Front Range, and a light cloud cover had rolled in off the Rockies keeping temperatures mild. I was grateful to not have to resort to Plan B, which was to find a corner of her well-appointed house to deposit the clawed devils in while we went out to eat.

A few words about those claws. I've come full circle on the issue, which isn't to say I wouldn't consider getting a kitten declawed, since they heal and adjust quickly at that age. Such was the case with the cats I had when married to Don, namely Arthur, Truman, and Murphy. I also had Sam declawed, even though he was about a year old when I got him.

But Jack was an indoor/outdoor cat and I couldn't even talk Mike into having him neutered, although fortunately someone in his inner-city neighborhood took that matter into their own hands before Jack moved to the suburbs. Then, out of necessity Jack's claws remained. Fig and Sauks were both grown cats, claws intact, by the time I got them, so when Andy came along, it was something of a moot issue.

My furniture has suffered accordingly. Jack was pretty good at using a scratching post, but Fig refused and Sauks quickly followed suit, apparently thinking: hey, wait a minute why do the rules apply just to me? It's a question I've asked myself and the only answer I can come up with is Mike had just died and I was in something of a give-a-shit mood.

Showing up at someone's door with a cat in tow is dicey at best and claws further complicate the matter. (If asked when checking into a hotel, I'd lie, figuring how much damage can they do in twelve hours.) So I was glad I didn't have to ask my aunt to find room for them even for just an hour or two.

This also meant I didn't have to backtrack after lunch, but rather keep heading west. My destination was Marcia's in the Vail Valley.

While parts of northern New Mexico are fraught with memories, it still feels new enough to make more. Colorado is the opposite. Too many of the formative years of my life played out in this landscape, including two of the largest disruptions: the move to Denver after college and then a dozen years later leaving my Denver home for the unknown possibilities of Texas.

Of all the Colorado highways of memory, I-70 heading west out of Denver probably ranks at the top. My first awareness of it dates back to 1968, when we were stuck in a construction traffic jam on our way back from a family mountain outing. My uncle, well into his cups, was behind the wheel.

"Who the hell is Buckleshoes?" he asked rhetorically, looking at a Ruckelshaus sticker that took up much of the bumper on the car in front of us.

The windows were down in the summer heat and a woman stuck her head out of the car to sharply inform him, "Ruckelshaus is the Republican candidate for senator of Indiana."

My uncle was momentarily taken aback before noting the much smaller Nixon for President bumper sticker next to it.

"Who the hell is Nixon then?" he shouted, a question that solicited no response as traffic started to move at that very opportune moment.

Five years later, Deputy Attorney General William Ruckelshaus would claim his five minutes of fame when he and his boss, Elliot Richardson, resigned rather than follow Nixon's orders to fire Watergate special prosecutor Archibald Cox.

Ruckelshaus was also the first head of the Environmental Protection Agency, but if he's remembered at all it will likely be for being a victim in what is now known as the Saturday Night Massacre.

I've been on I-70 thousands of times since my uncle exchanged taunts with some random Republican from Indiana. Those trips were with boyfriends and husbands, sisters and girlfriends, in summer and winter, first as a resident of Colorado and then as the despised Texas visitor.

One of the multitude of reasons Coloradoans dislike Texans is their lack of expertise in mountain driving. Interstate 70 has some serious inclines, and one has to either shift into overdrive or hit the gas hard to maintain seventy miles an hour. This is no problem for me. My dad taught me mountain driving back in the late 1960s and I've not lost the knack. Even after three decades of living in the flattest place on earth, I can cruise these roads without losing speed.

So Sauks and Andy and I started our climb, first up through the foothills, then past the cutoffs for Evergreen to the south and Central City to the north. We passed Idaho Springs, where I've had many a buffalo burger at the aptly named Buffalo Bar, and then wound through narrow canyons to Georgetown, which was another one of my common watering holes on this route.

Don and I used to spend Christmas at Copper Mountain. The first year we were crazy enough to bring the cats, who did not travel nearly as well as the ones I now had in the car. Poor Truman shit himself (as he was prone to do under the slightest hint of stress), causing Don to pull over in Georgetown and throw him in a snowbank.

I retrieved the poor animal and contemplated hitchhiking back to Denver with him zipped up in my ski parka, wondering who on all earth would pick up a woman who smelled like shit and was toting a cat. Fortunately, after a bit of cleanup under the cold-water tap of a mountain bar, Don let both of us back in the car. Have I mentioned my first marriage was not a particularly happy one?

Georgetown marks the beginning of the steep ascent to the Eisenhower Tunnel. Located at a little more than 11,000 feet, the tunnel is the highest point in the U.S. interstate system. It is also a little more than a mile and a half in length and occasionally the scene of some rather spectacular accidents.

That said, it does not have quite the gruesome history of the Mont Blanc Tunnel in the Alps, which is heavily regulated (only a few widely spaced cars at a time, very strict speed limits) after thirty-nine people died in its seven-mile-plus confines in a horrific fire in 1999.

The only restrictions in the Eisenhower Tunnel are a drop to a fifty-mile-per-hour speed limit and signs indicating that changing of lanes is not allowed. Both regulations are routinely ignored.

As we entered the tunnel, Sauks became distraught, I'm assuming because of the amplified noise. I tried not to let him distract me as he began to climb frantically over the piles of stuff I had crammed in the car to look first out one window and then another. He did get my attention, however, when I heard a rear window go down. Sauks had accidentally discovered the electronic window switch.

Holy shit. My life, or at least his, flashed in front of my eyes. In the heartbeat it took me to roll the window back up, I envisioned him jumping out of the car into the many oncoming headlights where he was sure to be flattened into gray-and-white roadkill.

There's no place to pull over in the tunnel and the sudden appearance of a cat would have likely resulted in a multi-car pileup in my wake. That would have been fun to explain to the authorities: Yes, I'm traveling with cats. Or was. Now it is cat in the singular. No, they weren't in carriers. Yes, I am an idiot.

Fortunately, Sauks did not take advantage of his momentary window of opportunity. "Lock the windows," I repeated aloud to myself over and over again as we exited the tunnel into Summit County.

Long, long ago I had a similar brush with fate. As I mentioned earlier, my Siamese cat Hershey was the supreme traveler. All I had to do to get him in the car was rattle my keys and he'd come running.

But on this occasion, we'd just traveled from San Diego to Denver and he'd had enough. I was somewhere in east Denver, making my way from downtown out to Aurora where I was staying with friends. It was a warm spring day and I had my window cracked about four inches.

In the middle of a busy intersection, I suddenly realized Hershey had somehow managed to squeeze through that narrow gap. All that remained of him in the car was his tail and one hind leg. I grabbed that leg and tail and somehow pulled him back into the car. Miracle of miracles, this maneuver was achieved while making a left-hand turn in a car with a manual transmission. Desperate times call for desperate measures.

Now I made the second half of my mountain journey buzzed on adrenalin. We were on the other side of the Continental Divide. Until Marcia moved to the Vail Valley, I had rarely traveled any further west than Copper Mountain. Since then, I've become quite familiar with Vail Pass, occasionally making my way through a snowstorm knowing the pass would soon close behind me.

I arrived at Marcia's mid-afternoon. She greeted me warmly as I transferred the cats to the bedroom in the walkout basement. Then it was the litter box. I have one that can be carried by its handle so I have no idea why back in Texas I'd grabbed one with a cover that doesn't latch and requires both hands. Another journey was made for their food and bowls.

Then I figured it was time for a glass of wine to calm my nerves, which were still jittery from the tunnel incident. My suitcase could wait.

Marcia and John were more than kind in letting me stay with them, because John is the most adamant cat hater I know. As far as he is concerned, cats kill songbirds and therefore should be exterminated off the face of the planet. End of argument.

Over the decades, John and I have had many a boozy fight over this issue. He is not to be dissuaded by pointing out my cats are strictly indoors, or that Europe's bubonic plague was partially due to the fact that the Catholic Church declared cats agents of the devil and had them slaughtered by the millions, which in turn resulted in an explosion of disease-carrying rats.

That bit of Black Death history is more complicated than the case I tried to make with many beers under my belt (John and I used to be prodigious beer drinkers). The church noted that cats seemed to be spreading the disease, and therefore deemed they were evil. While the former was indeed the case since they did carry the illness-inducing fleas, once the cats were gone the rat population increased exponentially, and since they were the primary transportation vehicle of the fleas, the plague got much worse instead of better.

Considering even the absence of rodent-spread plagues can't justify the existence of cats, it was extremely generous of John and Marcia to let my spawn of Satan under their roof. Sauks ventured up the stairs where he encountered their dog Ally in a hissy fit, so it was back to the basement for him. It was the first of five basement stays for Sauks and Andy during the month of August 2016.

Chapter 16: Scary neighbors

August 6: Edwards, Colorado, to Cody, Wyoming; 499 miles.

"Let me in you fucking cunt. Now!"

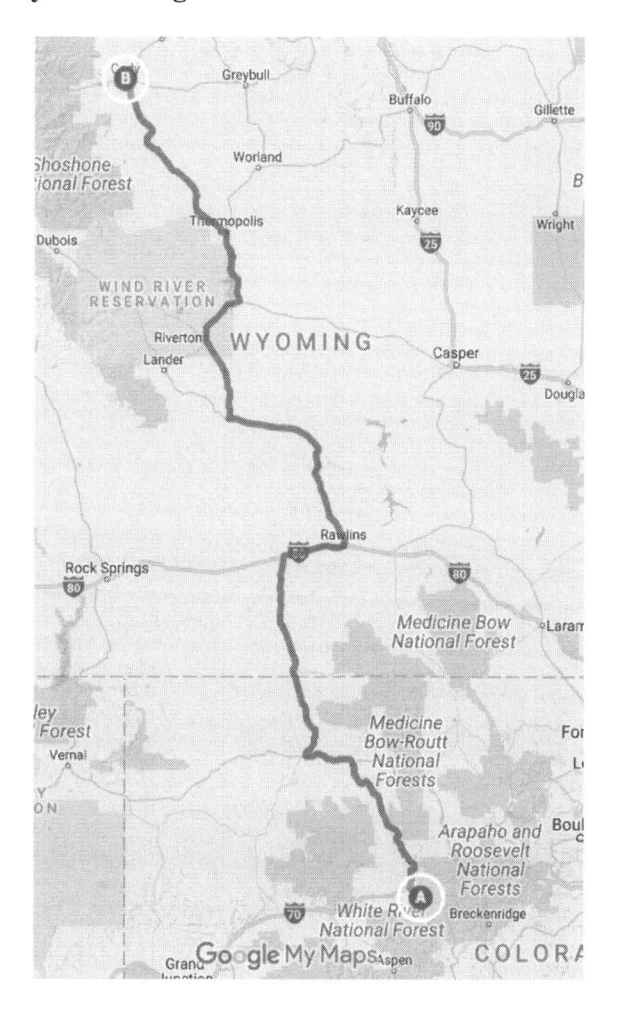

Sauks, Andy, and I looked at each other in alarm as our neighbor pounded on the door to the room next to ours, bellowing at the top of his lungs.

I'd noticed this creep and the "fucking cunt," who'd apparently locked him out, when they'd pulled up on their Harley an hour or so earlier. Both were decked out in black leather and chains. All exposed flesh—and there was plenty of it in strategic places—was patterned with tattoos and multiple piercings.

Now it appeared my initial revulsion held true: this book could indeed be judged by its cover.

A half an hour earlier, the tables had been turned. At that point, the "fucking cunt" was the one locked out.

"Open the goddamn door you bastard," she'd screamed, ice bucket in hand. Yes, the syntax and profanity were similar, but her soprano voice was more shrill than frightening. The deep, threatening tenor the cats and I were now listening to had all of our hair standing on end.

So much for the Big Bear Motel in Cody. I'd groaned when I'd pulled up earlier in the evening and saw I'd have to traverse a literal dog-and-pony show to reach the office. There was live cowboy entertainment consisting of an old coot on an electric keyboard with his sidekick dog. A sad-looking pony was pulling kids around the building in a small cart, while other assorted hooved animals stood by dejectedly watching.

Worst of all, there was a substantial crowd of seedy tourists gathered round witnessing this mess. I would have loved it as a child, laughed at it as a teenager, and been philosophical about it as a young adult, but now I was just grumpy.

With that uncanny feline instinct, Andy didn't want to get out of the car once I pulled up to our room. After multiple attempts to extract him from the kitty condo, I ended up just hauling it into the room with him firmly entrenched inside.

"Yeah," I said aloud, looking around our dark, shabby room. "I don't like it either."

As if the motel wasn't bad enough, how in the hell did I manage to time my first stay in Wyoming in longer than I could remember in the midst of Sturgis Week? The entire town was swarming with bikers.

I'm not a nervous traveler. I've landed in many a foreign country by myself. I've made my way through Delhi slums alone after dark, albeit not willingly; walked back to my hotel in Colombia after midnight unaccompanied; I've gotten in a random cab in Rio just hoping the driver would recognize the name of my destination I'd scrawled on a piece of paper.

In Nairobi, I jumped in a rusted-out car purportedly run by a local "tourist operator" who had approached my friend and me on the street. Once in the car, he'd pointed to a tiny, anonymous ad in a tourism brochure, dubiously claiming it was his.

Maybe it was the exotic nature of those risks—well I may die, but at least it will be interesting—that outweighed the fear I was now experiencing when confronted with your run-of-the-mill American of the gun-God-and-flag-toting variety.

Why hadn't I heeded Marcia's advice to check into their pet hotel of choice in this tourist town just east of Yellowstone National Park? My excuse is when it comes to traveling with pets, cat owners are not nearly as experienced as dog owners. It had been a long time since I'd had to deal with the challenge of finding lodging with an animal in tow. In the old days, I'd often plead ignorance or out-and-out lie.

When writing about Don and my Christmas trip to Copper Mountain, it occurred to me I have no idea whether or not that resort allowed pets; we just brought them.

On the move from Denver to Houston, Don and I checked into a West Texas motel with no intention of mentioning we had two cats lest they throw us out and we'd have to drive another fifty miles in the dark through flaring oil fields. When we discovered our room was right around the corner from the front desk, Don requested a room in the back on the flimsy excuse of wanting "more quiet." They obliged and we snuck Truman and Arthur through a back door in a Playmate cooler.

Since I wasn't working and did not plan to return before Labor Day to the third circle of hell known as Houston in summer, I had envisioned August 2016 consisting of leisurely travel. Instead my movement in the following weeks was more often than not dictated by the schedules of the family I was visiting. This required both accelerated travel and abbreviated stays in addition to being stranded for days on end when I would have much preferred to move on.

Such was the case at Marcia and John's, as I had only two nights with them before they had to travel to Denver for business. So that morning it was time to hit the road again.

Somehow the piles of stuff in my car seemed to be multiplying and finding a place for the litter box that was accessible for the cats lest they need it (which they never did) had become a challenge. Then I crammed my suitcase in the very back, before transporting one cat and then the other to the car.

All of this took multiple trips up and down the stairs.

"It is official," I told Marcia and John. "I am now obviously the craziest person in the family."

"You always were," John assured me.

Sauks, Andy, and I headed west on I-70 for seven miles before turning north on Colorado 131. My one and only sighting of a bear in Colorado happened on this stretch of road. Mike and I were making our way from Edwards to Fort Robinson, Nebraska, by way of Wyoming and were only a few miles up 131 when a black bear darted across the road, a cub on her heels. We pulled over to get a better look, which was a good call as she stood on her hind legs and beckoned a second cub to follow. It was both thrilling and a bit frightening, considering how much hiking I've done in this area—often alone.

Highway 131 crosses the Colorado River at the tiny hamlet of State Bridge. When I was a kid, my family would often camp in this area. On one of those trips, my drunken uncle stopped here for gas and other provisions. In the frigid mountain air of the previous night, we had been smoked like hams in a roaring pinewood fire that still failed to keep us warm. Consequently, the owner thought his store was on fire before determining the smell was coming from the passel of sooty kids rifling through his selection of candy.

I believe it was on that trip that Susan and I spent a night on the ground, fighting over an old quilt that was neither heavy enough nor big enough to shelter us from the bitter cold. I am happy to say that I have yet to spend another night as physically miserable as that one, including one after major surgery (hey, I had drugs and at least it was warm). It also says a lot about our upbringing that Susan and I knew it would have been pointless to complain about our extreme discomfort to any of the adults in the crowd.

Long-ago roommate and Hershey

Once past State Bridge, I continued up 131, skirting past Steamboat Springs. For all the time I've spent in Colorado, this was only the second time I could say I was in Steamboat. Once long ago a roommate and I visited it on a summer day trip, with Hershey in tow. Taking a cat along just because . . . what? As is the case with many things I did in my twenties, the logic now escapes me.

It goes without saying that I've never skied Steamboat, as it is relatively inaccessible from Denver. On my sole ski trip to Telluride in the southwestern corner of Colorado I recall a bartender noting that I'd driven by a half dozen "much better" ski resorts to get there.

A good illustration of how unserious a skier I was back in the day is the time I met a friend after work on a Friday for an overnight trip to Steamboat. There was a light, fluffy snow falling in Denver, so in an impromptu change of plans we opened a bottle of wine, lit a fire, and canceled our hotel room.

A nice evening in front of a warm fire watching it snow versus driving over an icy mountain pass after dark? That was a no brainer for someone not all that fired up to hit the slopes.

At Steamboat, I headed due west for forty-two miles on US 40, which is the shortest route between Denver and Salt Lake City, although most drivers choose I-70 to the south or I-80 to the north to avoid nearly 500 miles of two-lane driving through mountains.

At the town of Craig, I once again turned north on Colorado 13, which becomes Wyoming 789 just south of the tiny town of Baggs. I wanted to grab a bite to eat in Baggs, but found the one dining option seriously lacking in appeal. I've since read that because of its remoteness, Baggs was a renowned outlaw hangout in the 1800s.

My travel in Wyoming has been relatively limited, despite having lived in the adjoining states of Colorado and Nebraska. But I was now in a place where names were familiar due to years of writing about drilling activity in its multiple sedimentary basins. I cut my teeth on Rocky Mountain exploration in the 1980s, and I remember spotting wells from the towns of Wamsutter and Creston on oil and gas maps, as I drove through the Washakie Basin. At Creston, I took a short jog to the east on I-80 and then continued to make my way to the northwest on US 287.

Here I was driving through the Great Divide Basin, an arid, desolate landscape of red sand dunes dotted with antelope. This is where the Oregon Trail crosses the Continental Divide, an area that should have caused me to slow down and take stock of my surroundings, considering the books I've read in recent years on the subject including Rinker Buck's detailing of his 2011 journey in *The Oregon Trail: A New American Journey*, A. B. Guthrie's *The Way West*, and Francis Parkman's real-time account, *The Oregon Trail*, which was published in the 1840s.

(Regarding the latter, I was bemused that every time Parkman and his companion saw an interesting animal or bird, they killed it to get a closer look. But then, birdwatching was conducted in much the same way until the lenses of binoculars replaced the crosshairs of a hunting rifle.)

Sadly, as is usually the case when I'm traveling solo, I was hell bent on getting to my destination. Of course, technically I wasn't alone, but Sauks and Andy are not great conversationalists, unless you count Sauks's persistent meowing for at least the first hour or so of any day on the road. Furthermore, they cannot share with the driving and are not big on sightseeing, unless you count window hunting birds from a stationary perch.

So, I have no recollection of seeing the famous Oregon Trail landmark of Split Rock, although it would have been visible on the horizon to my left.

At Sweetwater Station, I veered off US 287 to the right and headed north through Riverton and Shoshoni. Then, with no warning or foresight, I was in the Wind River Canyon and it definitely caught my attention. Besides the steep canyon walls, white water, and the first green terrain I'd seen since leaving Colorado, I was struck by the frequent road signs identifying precisely what rock formation I was looking at. This is truly the state for geologists, I thought. In particular, I noted a sign identifying the Tensleep, a Pennsylvanian formation for which I'd pick log tops when writing about Wyoming wells.

That was back before my move to Houston and long before my transition to the international sector. At the time, everyone in my department was reading John McPhee's *Rising from the Plains*, a beautifully written tome on Rocky Mountain geology. Mind you, none of us were geologists. Some hiring manager had the harebrained idea that it would be easier to teach geology to writers than it would be training geologists to write. Okay, starting pay was probably also taken into consideration.

But, come to think of it, that humble beginning best sums up my years in the industry: an employment experiment that that got me lots of grief over the ensuing decades—until I learned to keep my mouth shut—and then finally backfired when it was probably a factor in the end my career. (Not that my sex and age didn't also come into play.) But such is life and I digress.

One of the things I remember best from McPhee's book was the explanation for the contrary paths of several notable Rocky Mountain rivers. The Wind River is a classic case. Against all logic, it flows north through a deep canyon that cuts through millennia of sedimentary rock. That's because this canyon was not formed by the river, but rather plate tectonics. The river predates the canyon and just stubbornly maintains the course it took when the landscape was relatively flat.

Once past the canyon, I felt like I was home free. Cody was about a hundred and twenty miles away. Maintaining a careful nine miles over the speed limit, I'd be there in less than two hours. With that thought, I looked in my rearview mirror and saw flashing red lights.

Fuck. God damn.

I pulled over on the shoulder as an RV I'd passed a bit earlier sped by. I could just imagine their glee: We'll get there before you, asshole.

I have never broken more than a minor traffic law, but for some reason cops instinctively dislike me. As a tall, lean Wyoming state trooper walked over to my vehicle, I carefully prepared my speech: "Here's my driver's license and registration. I can't keep my window down because I have cats in the car."

Fortunately, as I opened the window, neither cat came forward.

"Do you know what the speed limit is?" he asked.

What? Wyoming has speed limits?

I suppressed that smart-alecky answer. "Seventy?"

"Yes, and I clocked you at seventy-nine."

Really? Wow. How could you contain yourself?

I suppressed that reply as well. Instead, I told him about the cats.

"Will they try and get out?" he asked.

"Probably," I assured him.

He nodded, took my paperwork, and walked back to his cruiser. Only then did Sauks crawl in my lap.

I got off with a warning. Surprisingly, neither cat tried to escape when the window was once again lowered. Fear of cops perhaps?

I was still fuming at the inconvenience when about five miles up the road I came across a car that had just plunged into a steep ravine.

Since several other cars had already pulled over—and I had cats in the car—I cruised on by thinking, Mr. Trooper Man, you may have had bigger fish to fry than me.

Chapter 17: Dead Indians

August 7: Cody, Wyoming

If I were going to visit Yellowstone, which I wasn't, it wouldn't have been at the very peak of the tourist season, let alone the same week as the Sturgis Motorcycle Rally. Instead I was in Cody to see the Buffalo Bill Center of the West. I'd been introduced to it by my folks, who had taken us there on a trip to Yellowstone when I was in my early teens.

After finding a motel that was decent but cheap (never an easy task with four opinionated kids in the car), we made our way to the museum, spending an hour or so there before it closed. In a rare change of plans, Dad decided we had to go back the next morning, which delayed our arrival in Yellowstone by at least a half a day.

The museum visit itself wasn't out of the ordinary. Even when spending the night in some random town on the road, my father would check to see if there was some historical site we could hit before "supper." (My mother still has supper rather than dinner.) One that comes to mind was in a small Pennsylvania town where—in the dark confines of a few tiny, cluttered rooms—we came across a painting of a local Leonard who'd fought in the Revolutionary War. Could the family go back that far? Possibly.

I've wanted to return to Cody ever since that August day in the late 1960s. The Whitney Western Art Museum was one of the main reasons I'd yearned for decades to see it again. I remember vividly not only the Remington's and Russell's but the sweeping landscapes of Albert Bierstadt. Regarding the latter, I was intrigued by the notation that while his details of the western landscapes were fairly accurate, as a German he'd painted them in the "darker" hues of the European mountain ranges. It would be a half-life-time later before I would finally visit Europe and see the difference for myself.

On this visit, I was underwhelmed with the art museum. That Cody visit of long ago was probably my first glimpse of the works of true masters and since then I've seen a great deal of world-class art, including the vast array of Remington's and Russell's at the Amon Carter Museum of American Art in Fort Worth. In comparison, the collection in Cody seemed modest and very small.

The art was my first stop. Second was the Plains Indians Museum. Designated an affiliate of the Smithsonian in 2008, the Buffalo Bill Center is laid out like a wheel with five spokes. In addition to the Whitney and Indian sections, there are wings devoted to Cody's Wild West Show, the area's natural history, and firearms. Raised on television westerns ranging from *Rawhide* to *Wagon Train* to *Bonanza* to *Gunsmoke*, American Indians always fascinated me.

By the time my ancestors moved to Nebraska in the late nineteenth century, the reign—often of terror—of the noble plains tribes was over. But Native Americans still played a role in our lives.

I grew up on a farm on the Wayne-Thurston County line, which tripped up my cousin when she wrote in her father's obituary that he was born in Thurston County, which was the side they lived on. Ever the journalist, I pointed out he was actually born on the "home place" in Wayne County across the road.

Thurston and neighboring Dixon—I went to high school in the latter—are home to the Winnebago reservation. The Winnebago's were an eastern tribe that moved from Wisconsin to Iowa to Minnesota to South Dakota and finally to Nebraska. It is said they didn't thrive on the treeless plains of South Dakota and their reservation is now in the relatively wooded hills along the Missouri River in the very northeastern corner of Nebraska.

My crafty (or dishonest, depending on how you look at it) grandfather bought some of their land on the cheap. In the process, he got to know several members of the Winnebago tribe and they often visited our farm. I literally grew up with the warning to hide if the Indians showed up when I was home alone. Remember this was in the second half of the twentieth century. One of my mother's favorite admonishments was to behave or else she would pack us up and leave us on the doorstep of the Indians.

Since my family made a road trip to Denver every summer the crops were good enough to cover the expense, we were also exposed to what remains of the great tribes of the plains. As very small girls, Susan and I danced in what I assume was a Sioux powwow in the aptly named town of Ogallala. We were given names: Red Feather for her as she was sun burned from spending most of her waking hours outdoors, and Blue Sky for me, presumably because I was considerably paler albeit with brown rather than blue eyes.

I was a precocious child, often preferring to listen to adult conversations rather than play with the rest of the kids. On one of these occasions, I overheard a relative talking about the display of dead Indians in the Hastings Museum in south-central Nebraska. I was intrigued and insisted we stop to see them on our way back from Denver. My parents obliged, but I was extremely disappointed. Who knows what ghoulish display I expected, but the corpses looked like nothing more than dried-up roadkill to me. I'm sure these remains have long since been respectfully removed from Hastings in these far more politically correct times.

While the art museum in Cody was nearly as disappointing as the dead Indians, the Plains Indian Museum had expanded and made the two-night stay in the seedy biker motel well worth it. This collection of artifacts had begun— as did the museum itself—as something of a warehouse for items from Buffalo Bill's Wild West

146

Show. While the art took only a few minutes of my time, the Indian exhibits were so expansive, I took a break for lunch before I was half way through this wing of the museum.

My first stop was the Big Bear Motel to check on the cats. I'd told the not-terribly interested desk clerk I would not be requiring housekeeping that day. He looked oddly like the mountain man I'd encountered at the motel in Salida, Colorado, some weeks earlier, and had the same give-a-shit attitude.

"If you say so." He scratched my request down on a piece of lined notebook paper already filled with instructions of some sort, which did little to reassure me.

True to the nature of this dive, there was no do-not-disturb sign, and I envisioned Sauks and Andy escaping into the Wyoming wilds while a maid's cart was parked outside our open door. To my considerable relief, I instead found both cats sleeping on one of the two double beds. They were no doubt happy to have a day outside the confines of my Honda CRV, no matter how substandard the accommodations.

I had lunch at the historic Irma Hotel, which was built by Buffalo Bill himself and named for his youngest daughter. While the food was forgettable, the restaurant provided excellent people watching as it was packed with tourists as well as a number of actors or reenactors decked out in costumes and impressive displays of facial hair. Then it was back to the Buffalo Bill Center.

While in a museum, I always try and find at least one tidbit of information I didn't know and can hold onto. That afternoon, I learned mass-produced Venetian glass beads were a favorite trade item with the Indians in the nineteenth century and therefore rapidly replaced earlier decorations of bone, shell, and stone.

I love the symmetry of this fact: the many intricately beaded Indian artifacts I've seen in different museums since I was a small child were sourced in Venice.

A few years ago, one of my closest friends—whose lifelong ambition is to spend time in the American West—took me to Venice, a city she knows well as her mother was from the nearby Trentino-Alto Adige region. I have two necklaces of miniscule beads I bought on the island of Murano in the Venetian Lagoon.

But back to those pre-European decorations, in Cody I noted a child's dress made of trade cloth but decorated with elk ivory.

Just a few weeks earlier, my nephew gave me a piece of elk ivory he found while hiking in the mountains outside of Angel Fire, New Mexico. These nubby canine teeth—there's an oxymoron for you—are the remnants of tusks once grown by modern elk's prehistoric ancestors.

When I made it to the end of the Indian exhibits there was no time left for any of the other spokes, although I would have liked to have made at least a quick swing through the Buffalo Bill wing. I recall Mom saying William Cody bore an uncanny resemblance to a rather dashing neighbor of ours back in Nebraska.

It's no coincidence that Westerns have played such a large role in both movies and television. The end of the era of "cowboys and Indians" overlapped with the very beginning of the motion picture industry. Also, its California birthplace played a crucial role since the state not only lured so many across the frontier, it also provided both a cowboy culture and handy filming locations.

This is perhaps best illustrated in the opening sequence of *Butch Cassidy and the Sundance Kid,* which features frames from a silent movie. In the original cut of the film, Butch and Sundance watch themselves die on film just before they do indeed meet their fate.

But it was Buffalo Bill that turned the taming of the American Frontier into entertainment even while the likes of Sitting Bull and Annie Oakley were alive to participate in the show.

I need to return to Cody to see his wing of the museum. Next time I hope to avoid the bikers, leave the cats behind, and find better lodging.

Chapter 18: Heading east

August 8: Cody, Wyoming, to Chamberlain, South Dakota: 595 miles

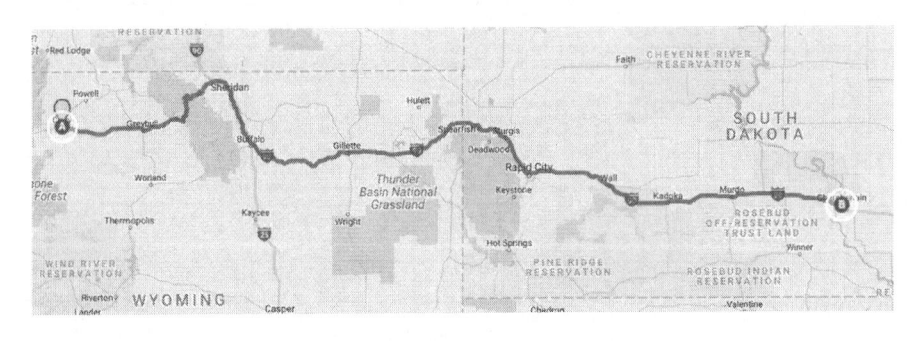

I was up before dawn on Monday morning. After quickly packing, I got on all fours to retrieve the recalcitrant cats, which at the first sign of a move had huddled under the bed closest to the far wall. It was on casters rather than a platform and I was not surprised to discover the floor beneath was filthy. Fortunately, all that remained of previous guests was one cast-off sock. I left the bed skewed, hoping housekeeping would take the hint and do some deep cleaning.

The office of the Big Bear Motel had just opened. I really didn't want to see the old mountain man again—he seemed to be the sole member of staff aside from housekeeping—but was desperate for caffeine and there was no coffee maker in my room. Unfortunately, the light brown liquid slowly dripping into a Mr. Coffee carafe in the lobby didn't smell good enough to justify the wait. I hit the road.

I was sorry to leave Wyoming so quickly, but my cousin Nancy wanted me to join her the very next morning in northeastern

Nebraska. I'd booked a room in Chamberlain, South Dakota, which would get me close enough to make it doable. By hitting the road so early, I hoped to fit in a quick one-or-two-mile hike in the Big Horn Mountains and still make the nearly 600 miles.

Sauks, bless his walnut-sized brain, had a different idea. As we headed due east, he began a persistent serenade. He would usually resign himself to a long ride in thirty minutes or so and shut up, but this time he wasn't giving up. So, to a background of nerve-grating meowing I retraced the tail end of my route two days earlier to Greybull via US 14 as the sun cleared the mountains ahead of me. Just past the town of Shell, I entered Shell Canyon. The scenery was spectacular. Sauks kept on crying, hoping to win some battle of wills.

Again, the drive was frequently punctuated with geologic markers. I stopped at a rest area where a sign informed me I was looking at Precambrian rocks 2.9 billion years old, making them among the oldest on earth.

As I drove up toward 10,000 feet, I conceded defeat to Sauks. No, I wouldn't pull over for a hike. There were extenuating factors: it was time to say goodbye to the mountains in particular and the West in general. I would spend the night on the wrong side of the one-hundredth meridian. It was going be a painful parting and I just needed to get it on with it.

With a heavy heart, I descended the steep drop down the eastern slope of the Big Horns. This range is unique in Wyoming in that it has thrust faults on both the west and east slopes, with no gentle dips on either side.

Long ago, my father drove us up the road I was now going down. I remember being frightened, perhaps because we had a clear view of our serpentine route to the top. For someone who strives to be in the high country and seeks out spectacular panoramas, I am occasionally struck with nearly paralyzing vertigo. Unfortunately, it follows no rhyme or reason.

Now, driving down toward Ranchester, I thankfully felt no such fear. However, I can easily recount other times my stomach clenched and my mouth went dry as I clearly envisioned imminent death: a nighttime drive down Lookout Mountain on the west side of Denver or once when Mike took a curve a bit too fast several hundred feet above the Pacific on Highway 1.

Sometimes I feel better when I'm driving, other times not. On a four-wheel route in the Four Corners, I was driving along a flat, rutted road, giving Don a cigarette-and-beer break (not that he wouldn't indulge in both while driving). Suddenly I was overtaken by a nail-biting fear, or would have been if I could have taken my hands off the wheel to gnaw on my fingers. Unbeknownst to us, we had been on top of a mesa and were now making our way down a cat walk.

I would have turned the wheel over to Don, but the track was too narrow to switch places without crawling over each other. My side was shoved up so closely against a cliff I couldn't fully open my door. On the other side, Don would have stepped into thin air.

"Jesus Christ! Look at all those crashed vehicles down there," he said.

Don was hanging out the window like a gleeful twelve-year-old boy.

It was physically impossible for me to look, but his proclamation did intensify my terror. When we once again hit level ground, I stopped so he could take over driving. As I shakily made my way to the passenger side, I resisted the urge to pause and kiss the ground.

A few miles beyond the Big Horns, I was on I-90, which would constitute the remaining 463 miles of my drive. Sauks was finally silent, Andy out of sight and mind in the kitty condo. I made a pact with myself to return to spend quality time in the Big Horns sometime in the future. It was my third time through these mountains. Between the present and teenage journeys, I once drove through with a friend from Denver on a road trip to Montana.

Another time I was rewarded with a spectacular view from above on a flight back from Calgary. It was a trip I made often during my international years in the oil and gas industry and I'd given up ever seeing any scenery justifying a window seat as the flight patterns typically go straight up the plains with the mountains out of sight to the west. But that time we were flying right above the peaks.

Besides their majesty, the Big Horns have historical significance. The Sioux and Cheyenne hid in these mountains after the battle of the Little Big Horn, knowing their victory over Custer was probably just a last hurrah. And the real Hole in the Wall is in the southern part of the range.

Speaking of that outlaw gang and Wyoming, the "Bolivian" scenes in *Butch Cassidy and the Sundance Kid* were filmed in Mexico. Therefore, the landscape depicted in the movie is relatively lush and tropical while in fact Butch and Sundance spent their final days in a high, dry Andean climate that looks much like Wyoming.

Another couple hundred miles down the road and I was in South Dakota. My siblings and I were always disappointed if our summer vacations took us no further than the state to the north, which was the case in years when it failed to rain enough for a good return on the spring planting.

Now, driving across South Dakota for the first time in more than forty years, I was struck by its beauty. Sturgis bikers aside, and there were plenty of them, I was enchanted by golden rolling plains and vast fields of sunflowers.

"Liquid or solid?" a volunteer asked me at a rest area east of Rapid City.

I'd stopped for a bathroom break, and noticed the free water being handed out by volunteers of a local Baptist church. Their objective was to keep the bikers hydrated, but I guessed—correctly—they'd give me one too.

When I expressed puzzlement at his question, he smilingly held up a bottle of water that was frozen solid. I opted for the liquid version.

The only other stop I made was for gas at Murdo, which I was mildly amused to find is a tourist attraction. People pause here in central South Dakota to visit the nineteenth century town that was constructed as a movie set for *Dances with Wolves.*

I was not tempted to see it. Not only was I anxious to get the cats to our evening destination, but I was feeling somewhat blue because I was heading eastward and downhill. The elevation was dropping toward the 2,000-foot mark and the humidity was rising.

I crossed the hundredth meridian going the wrong direction at Presho. Forty miles later, I reached my predetermined destination of Chamberlain, a town of 1,400 that sits at the junction of I-90 and the Missouri River. A sign on the interstate informed me it was also the exit for the Lewis and Clark Information Center.

After checking the cats in to the AmericInn and a dinner of Buffalo wings at a pizza place near the river, I drove to a spot overlooking the Missouri that had been the site of an encampment of the Corps of Discovery. The interpretation center was closed for the evening, so I simply stood on the bluff and longingly looked toward the west from whence I'd come.

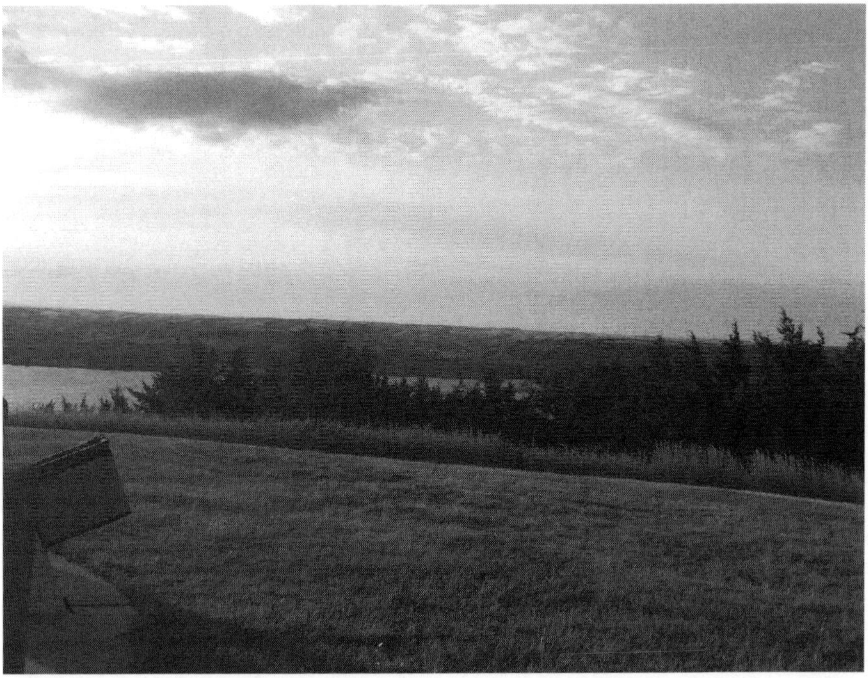

Part 4: The long road home

Chapter 19: God's Country and Grandma's

August 9: Chamberlain, South Dakota, to Wayne, Nebraska: 212 miles

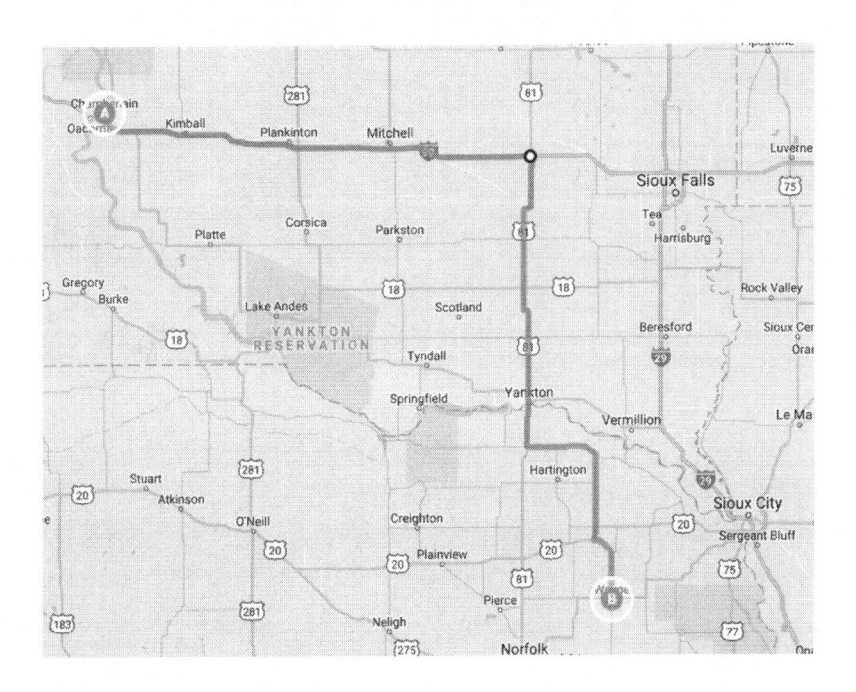

Where the hell was that damn cat?

Sauks had already been herded into a carrier, which resulted in Andy pulling a vanishing act. So before fully addressing the Andy issue, I started hauling everything else out to the car.

I took Sauks down on the last trip. After I deposited his carrier on the floor on the passenger's side, I reached into the center console for a flashlight. There are only so many places to hide in a motel room and I'd checked them all save one: the four-inch gap I'd discovered between the platform bed and the wall.

Once back in my now-empty room, I got down on the floor with a groan and craned my neck. I was looking for a black cat in a dark motel room on the one morning I absolutely had to be on the road before sunrise. After a bit of difficult maneuvering, I shot the flashlight down the narrow space and was rewarded with the glow of two green eyes looking back at me.

Son of a bitch. Figuring the bed was probably quite heavy, I envisioned running down to the front desk to get someone to help me move it. Would there be more than one person on duty at five a.m.? How long would the whole process take? I needed to be in Wayne no later than nine-thirty.

Fortunately, this whole line of thinking was unnecessary. I gave the bed a hard shove and it moved just enough for me to wedge my body behind it. This quick sequence of events distracted Andy for the few moments it took to grab him.

The little shit curled into a tight ball in my arms and we went out to the car and got on the road without further incident.

After that first day leaving Sugar Land two months earlier, I'd decided cramming Sauks's thirteen uncooperative pounds into a carrier while still in the cramped confines of the CRV was unnecessary. Unlike Andy, his reaction was curiosity rather than fear, perhaps because of his years as an indoor/outdoor cat. Therefore, it wasn't too hard to hang onto him, even while figuring out which type of motel key card I had in my hand.

The night before, Sauks had been the first thing to be deposited into my room at the AmericInn in Chamberlain. I propped the door open a crack with the safety lock and returned to the car for Andy. On the return trip, Andy and I were greeted by a white paw sticking through the opening.

No matter how many times I'd do this in the coming weeks, I never could get it down to less than four trips: First one cat, then the other, then the litter box, then their bag of food and bowls. Sometimes I could handle the latter while pulling my suitcase, but by that time why bother? It was enough to make me yearn for a dog.

On trip three or four in Chamberlain, Sauks got past me and ran down the hall. Fortunately, he made a left-hand turn away from the lobby, which was to the right and close enough to be visible from my doorway. Nonetheless, it took a while to corner his furry gray ass in a cubby hole under the stairs to the second floor.

That's when I decided it was back to carrier transportation for Sauks.

The following morning, there was just a glimmer of light on the horizon as we headed east on I-90. Within an hour, I passed the exit for Mitchell and smiled. It was not amusement at the memory of stopping to see the Corn Palace on one of those despised South Dakota vacations, but rather Mike's horror when I confessed I'd been there. I don't recall what he was watching on television that featured the Corn Palace. Believe me, it's not that interesting.

I was now in a part of the U.S. I find more culturally disorienting than many foreign countries, despite having spent the first twenty-four years of my life on the upper plains.

By the time I turned south on US 81 for the final run into Nebraska, the sun had come up. Or would have if there hadn't been an early morning cloud cover. The dry air of the west was behind me and a heavy mist was roiling out of the corn fields. I was still more than thirty miles from Yankton when I felt an urgent call of nature.

If worse comes to worse, I thought, I can take cover in those corn fields. Fortunately, there was a Casey's General Store in Freeman (population 1,274 as of 2014, a decline of 32 souls from the 2010 census) that was not only open at this early hour, but also busy. As nonchalantly as possible I made my way through a group of men getting ready to go to work somewhere nearby.

The women's restroom was unoccupied and—this being God's country as any resident of these parts will tell you—very clean. On the way out, I bought a cup of coffee, more out of courtesy than thirst or need for caffeine.

I stepped outside into the midst of men smoking and idly watching Sauks, who was crouching on the dashboard. This was no doubt the oddest thing they'd seen in a while: a woman traveling alone, with Texas tags and a cat. No, wait a minute. Make that two cats. Uncharacteristically, Andy had crawled out of the kitty condo and joined Sauks on the dashboard.

I had to bat them aside when I got in, not an easy endeavor with a cup of hot coffee in my hand.

"Don't worry, boys," I said aloud. "Just a couple hours to go, and then you're going to have a whole house to explore."

We were headed to Grandma's.

Chapter 20: There's no place like Wayne

August 10: Wayne, Nebraska

"Sounds like a cat jumping down from the counter."

I had to give Mom credit. For a woman pushing eighty-eight-years old, her hearing was excellent. The soft staccato two-beat thud had been the only sound in the house other than the ticking of a clock. And yet, it had failed to register with me. But then I hear it all the time, while Mom was all too aware of the furry, four-legged animals that had invaded her house.

Andy wasn't making any friends here. There was zero chance of him winning over Mom's heart to begin with; she is a farm woman who has never veered off her upbringing that animals are livestock. In other words, they can be a good source of food and income or keep rodents and other pests at bay, but have no place beyond that. Letting them in the house is big-city nonsense.

Now Andy was sabotaging any microscopic hope he had of making peace with his endless exploration of the upper reaches of her home and periodic grazing in her expansive indoor garden of African violets.

We'd arrived in Wayne, Nebraska, shortly after nine the previous morning, giving me just enough time to make the multi-trip transfer to Mom's basement plus a few more minutes to try and look presentable for my day's outing with my cousin, Nancy.

Fortunately, the original owner of Mom's house had converted the basement into an apartment, so Sauks and Andy were left behind a closed door, denying them access to the rest of her domain. But when I was present, I'd let them upstairs just long enough for them to cause trouble, at which point they were quickly herded back down into the basement.

The granting of freedom followed by exile had become something of a game, but at least Sauks and Andy were getting some much-needed exercise. They'd spent two months in our tiny casita and since then a fair amount of time cramped in a car. They deserved the widest latitude of freedom I could muster under the circumstances.

At this stage of my journey, my movements were being dictated by the needs and plans of family. The day before, I'd gone with Nancy to her attorney's as she was at long last settling her father's estate. My uncle Roy, who had passed away the previous October, was my father's youngest brother and last surviving sibling. They had farmed together, living a quarter mile apart on opposite sides of the Thurston-Wayne county line.

Nancy was born nine months before me and we grew up together, more like sisters than cousins. Over the years, our relationship has waxed and waned a bit, but we make a mutual effort to connect beyond the miles. She lost her only sibling four decades earlier to cancer, so on this sad occasion I was determined to be there for her, even if it meant leaving the mountains sooner than I would have liked.

My roots run deep in northeastern Nebraska. I grew up here on the edge of the west, or if you look at it from the other direction, the beginning of the fertile country that comprises the corn belt.

My father died in 1994 on the same piece of real estate he'd been born on eighty-one years earlier, nearly equidistant from where the Missouri River separates Nebraska from South Dakota to the north and forms the Iowa state line to the east. Both of his grandfathers had settled in this bend of the river in the 1880s. Mom's forebears arrived a few years after his, albeit from Germany rather than a couple states back east.

I was born in Wayne in the Benthack Hospital, which was named for the town doctor. Now the police station although its old name is still engraved in granite above the doors, it is just a few blocks from where Mom lives. This town was our epicenter, located between Mom's hometown of Winside and the Leonard family farm about twenty miles to the east.

Wayne has a population a bit beyond 5,000, which makes it one of Nebraska's larger towns. I told Mike this once, to which he replied, "Are you kidding me? You walk five blocks in any direction and you're in a corn field."

About nine out of ten towns in Nebraska have less than 3,000 people, with hundreds clocking in below 1,000. This is a distinction the state shares with North and South Dakota to the north, Kansas and Oklahoma to the south, and Iowa to the east. It is a unique place, but because finding another world entails more than a day's drive, many people who live here do not fully comprehend it. And those who do, like my mother, still often suspiciously regard outsiders as either snooty, misguided, or just dead wrong (and sometimes all the above).

It is easy to recount the steps I took from the farm to the fourth largest city in the country and an international career. I made my way from a one-room country school to a high-school graduating class of thirty-nine in a neighboring town, and then on to Lincoln where some 25,000 mostly rural kids congregated at the University of Nebraska. It wasn't until my junior year in college that I got on a plane for the first time. After college, I escaped to Denver, which was the first true city I lived in. A dozen years later I took a job transfer to Houston.

The hard part is comprehending the changes I went through to adapt to the world beyond insular rural Nebraska. Fortunately, I inherited wanderlust and curiosity about the outside world from both of my parents, which paved my way.

One of my favorite childhood memories is of riding with Dad the night before one of our annual family vacations.

"I wonder where we'll be by this time tomorrow," he mused as he studied the soybean field we were passing. "Farming" by car at dusk was a summer ritual.

Going back to the upper Midwest always results in a case of profound culture shock coupled with stifling boredom.

There's a scene in the movie *Terms of Endearment* where John Lithgow asks Debra Winger if she misses Texas. They are supposedly in Iowa, but the scene was filmed outside of Lincoln. Her character says something to the effect there is a wildness about Texas she misses.

This sums up my reaction to Nebraska. Simple human nature dictates the state has its share of drama and dysfunction, but it is still the most sugar-coated place I've ever been. It can be as sticky sweet as the Snickers salad (no, you didn't read that wrong, Google it) served in the church basement after my uncle's funeral.

A college friend sends me *Nebraska Life* every year for Christmas. The letters to the editor are all positive and overly sentimental: "There really is no place like Nebraska." I'm hoping that my son "will get homesick enough that when he retires from the military, he will move home to Nebraska."

Contrast that magazine with *Texas Monthly*. Admittedly, they are in different genres, but I can't imagine anything like it ever coming out of Nebraska. In addition to its glossy ads for Neiman Marcus and other merchants of high-end luxury goods, *Texas Monthly* always features at least one article on some stupefying local politics, another on a horrid example of social injustice, and for good measure, often a long investigative piece on a particularly gruesome crime.

In comparison, Nebraska is monochromatic. True in the summer the eastern half of the state—thanks to irrigation to supplement the rains which can be a bit dicey this far west—is vibrant green. But once the crops are harvested and the trees bare, Nebraska is nearly as colorless as Alexander Payne's black-and-white movie of the same name

A number of people I knew growing up moved away only to return to Nebraska some years later. I can't imagine it. Some years back, I ended a visit to Nebraska with a business trip to New York, catching an early-morning flight from Omaha to La Guardia. Upon landing, I realized as I elbowed my way through the crowds that I felt comfortable for the first time in a week.

So, time in Nebraska is always spent trying to behave myself, being mindful of the feelings of the people around me, and not acting like a big city snob. My snubbing of Snickers salad is a prime example, which reminds me: I would love to drop that snooty bitch Ann Coulter into this world to see just how much she likes spending time with the audience she plays to.

Fortunately, on this trip I was soon to be joined by my sister Susan, her daughter Ariel, and Ariel's Irish husband, Anthony.

If there is a perfect antidote for Nebraska, it is Anthony. A visit to Ariel's Nebraskan grandparents—my brother-in-law hails from Ueling several dozen miles south-southeast of Wayne so she has a total of three in the state—wasn't his first exposure to this part of the country. A mid-distance runner, Anthony came to the U.S. on an athletic scholarship that landed him at Central Iowa Community College in Fort Dodge.

I can't imagine what Anthony's initial impression of Iowa must have been. He'd spent his eighteen years to date in the southern Dublin suburb of Tallaght, which as an aside means plague pit or grave in Irish, although thankfully no ancient mass graves have been unearthed there—at least yet. But then Anthony could probably adapt to life on Mars, so the corn belt probably presented few problems. After two years in Iowa he was picked up by the University of Arkansas track-and-field team and moved to Fayetteville. That's where he met Ariel, who is pole vaulter.

Ariel and Anthony were on a mission. They'd been married by a judge a year earlier to keep him from being deported and were now planning a proper wedding celebration. My brother, a Lutheran pastor, had agreed to officiate. Family or not, Pastor Charlie takes his role seriously and had summoned them to Minnesota for bit of couple's consultation. Along with Susan, Ariel and Anthony were swinging through Nebraska on the way up. Everyone except me was on a narrow time frame.

Despite the slow ticking of the clock in my mother's otherwise silent house, my travel was still on fast forward. There were a couple friends I'd hoped to visit while in Nebraska, but those plans were scrapped. On Friday Sauks, Andy, and I would join our three new travel companions and head north.

Chapter 21: A basement birthday celebration

August 11: Wayne, Nebraska

Everything in Wayne is technically within walking distance as the town encompasses not much more than a square mile. But, my mother and my cousin live only a block apart, which makes bouncing back and forth between their houses especially convenient. It echoes the circumstances of my childhood, before our parents moved off the farm when our families were separated by a short stretch of unpaved road. Back then, we freely came and went between houses, entering without so much as a knock.

It would be hard to exaggerate how close we were. A fluke of geography kept us separated during elementary school since we were, as I've mentioned, on different sides of the county line. But by the time we left our one-room country schools for Wakefield High, our paths were thickly entwined.

Among my earliest memories are two that I believe were my initial interactions with my cousins. The first is sitting on my father's lap in the storm cellar.

"Those are your cousins," he told me pointing to two girls who were not much older than me. They were sitting on newspapers laid down to protect them from the damp subterranean floor. I know from family lore it was during a particularly stormy spring when we spent so much time in that underground room, furniture had been hauled down for our comfort. However, there still weren't enough chairs for all our guests.

"Their names are Barb and Nancy," he continued.

It may have been on that very night that my aunt and uncle were chased up the road by a tornado that fortuitously rose to spare our houses before bouncing over Logan Creek and hitting the farms of my father's other two brothers to the east.

I grew up with the conviction, no doubt strengthened by annual spring viewings of *The Wizard of Oz*, that it was just a matter of time before that tornado returned to finish the job. I came to view this as childhood nonsense, only to see history repeat itself in 2014 when a twister destroyed all the homes of my grade school classmates one mile to the west. Once again, the old farmhouse I grew up in was spared.

My other early memory of my cousins is the first time Susan and I went to their house alone. As is often the case in Nebraska, it is also weather related. A late-spring downpour had turned our road into a sea of mud, which is perhaps the reason Susan and I, despite being hardly more than toddlers, walked to our cousin's birthday party rather than being driven. Mom carried us, one by one, across the road. Then she stood and watched as we carefully navigated the relatively passable grass on the shoulder in our tiny red rubber boots. The sun was shining brightly and the air was heavy and wet. Susan and I turned around frequently as Mom's white blouse became smaller and smaller in the bright emerald world surrounding her.

I'm fairly certain it was mid-June and therefore Barb's birthday, because Nancy's birthday falls in August, when the rains are less frequent and the landscape not quite so verdant. Barb died of lymphoma shortly after her twenty-fifth birthday in 1976. Nebraska has a particularly high incidence of lymphoma and a link has been made with agricultural herbicides, so it is quite likely that Barb tragically drew the short straw in our family. Thirty-eight years later, her mother (my dear Aunt Ruth) died of lung cancer having never smoked a day in her life.

Nancy's birthday also called for a celebration, albeit one dampened slightly by the approaching end of summer and the beginning of the next school year. The most memorable was the one when she opened a jar of milkweed pod pickles she'd expressly saved for the occasion. Aunt Ruth was a school teacher with little time for gardening and the subsequent canning and freezing of fruits and vegetables. So, Nancy was fascinated by our vegetable garden and all the food preparation that went along with it. No doubt taking a clue from watching Mom make pickles, a few weeks before her birthday she'd packed the pods in a jar, added water and, for good measure, threw in a horse turd. Like mud pies, producing something edible was not the intent. But neither was the explosion of fermented plant and animal matter that resulted in the indignity of a second bath in a single day. Nancy's birthday pickles became the stuff of family legend.

While my current trip to Nebraska had been moved up due to Nancy's appointment with her attorney, it also happily coincided with her birthday. The Arkansas family had arrived the night before and by late afternoon I decided I'd spent enough time catching up with them and excused myself to walk up the alley and around the corner to Nancy's.

While Mom's house is a classic brick ranch—I recall watching it being built as we drove past on our way to church in the early 1960s, never dreaming someday it would be ours—Nancy's is a mission-style wood-frame from an earlier era. And, rather than being located on the highway that dissects Wayne into north and south halves, it is situated on prime real estate overlooking Bressler Park, named for a town founder who happens to be one of our ancestors (Bressler was my paternal grandmother's maiden name).

Nancy's home is resplendent with antiques, original artwork, hardwood floors, and leaded glass. But somehow we always end up in the man cave, a semi-finished, basement room furnished with cast-off furniture located at the bottom of a steep flight of steps. Her husband and his black lab joined us as we partook of a few birthday toasts and, since I'd recently been in Colorado, a few birthday tokes.

In the haze of marijuana smoke, Nancy decided to go upstairs and take a bath.

"Looks like it's going to rain," her husband said. "So, I guess I'd better walk the dog."

All three disappeared, leaving me alone to reminisce about the Christmas night Mike and I had joined them in this very room. It was my first time "home" for Christmas in more than three decades and Mike's last Christmas on earth. He had been darkly amused by the combination of Salem cigarettes, Windsor Canadian, and Diet Pepsi.

"Who says Nebraska doesn't have culture," I laughed on the short, sub-zero walk back to Mom's.

I came back down to earth (actually beneath it) wondering how Nancy's husband knew it was going to rain since we were so far underground no daylight to speak of could filter through the one narrow-slit window at ceiling level. Since neither of my hosts were present, the logical thing to do was to leave. But a loud clap of thunder stopped me in my tracks halfway up the stairs. I proceeded to the door on the landing and was rewarded with a front-row seat to a first-class Nebraska summer storm.

This brought about another basement memory. It was 1979 and I'd come home to the farm for my brother's wedding a day or two earlier. I was catching a flight out of Omaha the next morning and had gone to bed early only to be awoken by the wraithlike figure of my mother in a thin summer nightgown.

"It's a bad storm," she said calmly. "Come to the basement."

Do I have to? I remembered thick cobwebs and God knows what else two floors below me. The worst errand in my childhood was the directive to go to the basement and retrieve a specific fruit or vegetable. When it was my turn, I'd descend with goosebumps and deep sense of foreboding only to be confronted with a vast array of home-canned goods indistinguishable from one another because they were draped in a heavy coat of dust, some of which was produced by the ancient-but-still-in-operation coal furnace around the corner. I'd run back upstairs praying that the jar I clutched was the right one and I wouldn't have to make the dreadful journey a second time.

But the wind and rain thrashing at the window dissuaded me from arguing on this occasion. So, I huddled with Mom and Dad and my wide-eyed California boyfriend near the coal furnace, just outside the entrance to the cave. That grim space had long been given up to collapsing earthen walls and salamanders, but would still offer refuge if the house were to be lifted—Dorothy style—off its foundation.

"Hey there."

My reverie was interrupted by the appearance of Nancy's son, Marcus.

"Where is everybody?"

"Your mom's taking a bath and your dad is out walking the dog. Hope he found cover somewhere."

"Well, since they're not here, I'm going to head on home. Do you want a ride?"

"It's only a block," I demurred.

"Yeah, but all hell's broken loose out there."

So, Marcus gave me my one and, to date, only ride back to Mom's from Nancy's. I was damn glad for it.

Chapter 22: Other people's plans

August 12: Wayne, Nebraska

"What the feck is all this shite?" Anthony was more than a bit annoyed.

As if I didn't already have way too much in my car, I was now trying to add some artwork.

I'd pulled everything out of the Honda upon my arrival at Mom's in an attempt to consolidate and organize. All I'd really achieved was losing my car key. Thankfully I had a spare.

So now with Anthony, Susan, and Ariel's assistance, all this "shite" was once again being pulled out and rearranged.

"Keep an eye out for that key," I instructed.

The art in particular had Anthony fuming. Both Susan and I had several large framed pieces. I was hoping mine could somehow be crammed in on top of my bicycle and camping gear.

"Do you really have to have this stuff?" he kept asking, despite my repeated explanations that these were family treasures.

The day before, Nancy had graciously invited us to her father's house to see if there was anything we wanted among the stacks of oils, watercolors, and silkscreen prints stored in his basement. My cousin is an art teacher, and while some of the works were hers, a surprisingly large number were Barb's. The remainder were my Uncle Roy's.

Like my father, my Uncle Roy's first career choice had not been farming. Dad wanted to be an attorney, but the Great Depression and his role as the oldest son on a family farm that needed his attention got in the way.

Uncle Roy was the artistic one in the family. The only one of my father's siblings to get a college education, he was a high school music teacher for some years before returning to farm. His hobby was painting, a passion he shared with both of his daughters.

There seemed to be a bit of something for everyone in Uncle Roy's basement. I took two of Barb's oils for my office plus a charcoal abstract of hers I'd have to find a place for. By this time, I could hardly remember what my house in Texas looked like, let alone what was hung where.

Unlike his daughters, Uncle Roy had no formal training, which isn't to say he didn't have some nice pieces. Mom found a vividly colored rooster that was perfect for her kitchen. Susan chose a seascape, while I selected a small oil of a rippled lake nestled in lush pine-covered hills. I would venture both of the latter were inspired by trips he and my aunt took back east once they'd retired.

To the background of Anthony's loud Celtic curses, I gave up and begged Susan to take some of my stuff, including the three framed prints, in her Honda Pilot. I'd retrieve them on some future trip to Arkansas.

We weren't yet at the mid-point of August and I'd already realized that living out of a car is no fun. Sauks and Andy, at the moment cowering behind a closed door in the bedroom of Mom's basement, could not have agreed more.

To automatically put the words "Irish" and "pub" in the same sentence is not a cliché. On my multiple trips to Ireland, if someone back home asked by text or email, "Where are you?" the answer was invariably, "In a pub."

Anthony will find a pub, or the sorry American equivalent, wherever he goes. Fortunately, we had an excellent choice in Wayne: The Broken Antler. As we were leaving town, I parked the car a block away, under an elm tree so the cats wouldn't cook. It was our third visit to the Broken Antler in thirty-six hours. Or was it our fourth?

The Broken Antler, which had been recently opened by Marcus, is located in a tiny building between Arnie's Ford and Flowers & Wine. Did I say nothing interesting ever happens in this part of the country? Forget that. Fifteen years earlier, Flowers & Wine was the scene of a kidnapping right out of *Pulp Fiction*. Google "Wayne Nebraska Flower" and the story will pop right up.

A previous owner of this gift shop lured a man from Houston on an Internet hook-up site and then held him captive in a basement cell for nine days. This poor victim was sexually tortured before a second man, who'd also participated in these vile acts, helped him escape.

This is a horror movie waiting to be made. It would open as this poor Houstonian drove north through Oklahoma and Kansas, the population becoming sparser and sparser the further north he went. And that was only the beginning of his nightmare.

"This is Mom's family," Marcus told a regular while mixing a drink. "Dad's family isn't nearly this much fun."

Since it was only mid-morning, there was room for all four of us around the bar. I ordered a Bloody Mary, which was served with a stick of beef jerky rather than a stalk of celery—a nice Nebraska touch. We were joined shortly by Nancy and her daughter-in-law, Lacey.

We were having a farewell drink, at least those of us who weren't pregnant like Lacey, or driving which thankfully included me. Susan had graciously offered to let me ride shotgun on our impending drive to Minnesota. Our destination was my brother's lakefront cabin, Idaway, outside Alexandria in the northwestern part of the state. We'd briefly considered going to North Dakota as Pastor Charlie is a busy man and didn't seem anxious to see us just quite yet.

"There's got to be something to see in Fargo, right?" I asked my new travel companions. "That will put us within a couple hours of Alexandria. And I've never been to North Dakota."

Yes, I still have this childhood obsession of checking off states I've visited. I'm down to three: Alaska, North Dakota, and South Carolina. Two of the three are ironic. With the tiniest bit of effort, I could have easily arranged a work-related trip to Alaska, but somehow never got around to it. The fact I've never set foot in North Dakota is even odder as I've literally been within biking distance while visiting the Minnesota clan. Once—to hoots of derision from the northerners—Susan and I said we were going to drive up I-94, cross the state line and return. We found something better to do, although I don't remember quite what it was.

This time I'd even gone so far as to book a hotel room in Fargo. But then Charlie changed his plans to accommodate us and we were now headed for Lake Ida.

We said a final goodbye to our Nebraska cousins and got on the road before too much alcohol was consumed.

Chapter 23: I still don't make it to North Dakota

August 12: Wayne, Nebraska, to Alexandria, Minnesota: 355 miles

This time we got so close to North Dakota it was ridiculous. When we turned off I-29 in the very northeastern corner of South Dakota and headed east into Minnesota, we were within a running distance of about six miles.

Admittedly, this route added a dozen or so miles to our journey as I-29 veers to the west once past the town of Brookings, but we wanted to stay on the interstate as long as possible to take advantage of its eighty-mile-per-hour speed limit.

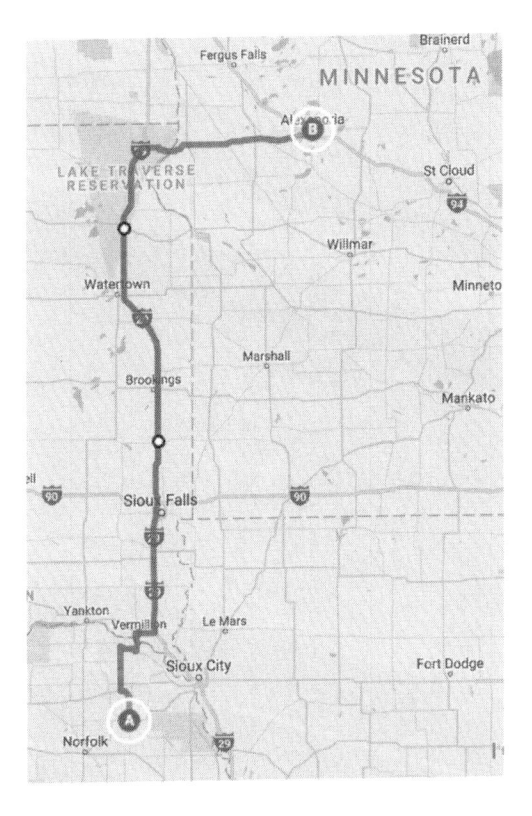

The trip began with a drive straight north out of Wayne on Nebraska State Highway 15. This was the route I'd taken into Wayne a few days earlier. We drove through Laurel, a town of 1,000 people that was the birthplace of actor James Coburn, although he wasn't there long. Coburn's father lost his business in the Great Depression and moved the

183

family to California while James was still an infant. His movie-star features were no doubt partially inherited from his mother, who was a Swedish immigrant.

There's a common Nebraska thread in this story: good-looking, talented people of Northern European descent who leave the state and find fame and fortune in motion pictures. Think Fred Astaire, Henry Fonda, and Marlon Brando in Hollywood's Golden Age up to Andrew Rannells today.

Highway 15 dead ends at Highway 12, an east-west route that parallels the Missouri River. On Tuesday, I had crossed the river at Yankton to the west. Now we turned east toward the relatively new Newcastle-Vermillion bridge, which was completed in 2001. We were in loess hills, Pleistocene wind-blown silt deposits along the Missouri that are generally too steep to farm and make for a lush and pretty landscape.

I felt a bit guilty as we turned back north a few miles shy of the town of Newcastle to make our way into South Dakota. The college friend who sends me *Nebraska Life* every Christmas lives in a converted grocery store on Newcastle's Main Street. I'd planned to see Joey, but my Nebraska stay had been cut short by family obligations.

Interstate 29, which dissects the eastern edge of South Dakota from north to south or in our case from south to north, is a largely uneventful drive. Anthony and Ariel, following in Susan's Pilot, attempted to alleviate the boredom with frequent calls, but none of us had much to say.

Sauks, on the other hand, was restless. He was used to me being behind the wheel, where the most response he'd solicit was a hard shove. Now that I was unoccupied in the passenger seat, he had a more participatory target and made frequent, disruptive visits to the front seat. Unfortunately, he still felt some compulsion to bother the driver, so I was continually running interference.

Susan has a Savannah cat, Georgia, who is occasionally transported from one part of Arkansas to another. Even with drugs, poor Georgia loses control of her digestive system, resulting in effusive emissions from both ends. So, Susan was philosophical about Sauks's non-liquid machinations.

Once off I-29, we crossed over Lake Traverse into Minnesota. At Herman, population 437, we entered a landscape pockmarked with countless bodies of water carved out by receding glaciers. Many of these are little more than a pond and don't warrant a name. We were indeed in the Land of 10,000 Lakes.

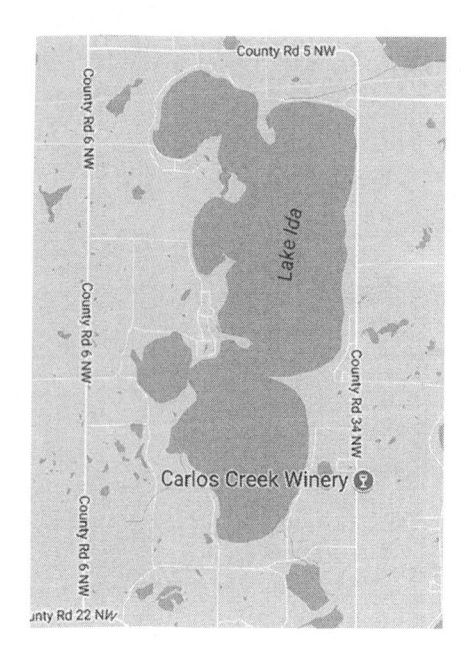

Located north of Alexandria, Lake Ida is one of the larger in the area. When viewed on a map, it bears an odd resemblance to a headshot of Abraham Lincoln looking to the west. We'd be staying on the back of Abe's head at about eye level.

Once through Alexandria, we watched for the tiny weathered sign in the ditch to the left that designates the entrance for the Idaway cabin. We found it on first try and Charlie's Honda Odyssey was already at the end of the long tree-lined driveway.

"Anne! Control your damned cat."

For the second time that day I was being yelled at in a heavy Irish brogue.

I abruptly abandoned my glass of wine and made a mad dash down the stairs. Andy was in a hissing, growling standoff with Charlie's cat, Ted, beneath one of the beds in the basement.

"Andy is an asshole," Anthony added for good measure as I grabbed my angry ball of black fur. I couldn't argue; it was back to the crypt for the little beast.

I had the basement bedroom at Idaway, largely so I could lock the cats in with me if need be, which indeed proved to be the case—at least for Andy. This was Ted's home away from home and he wasn't about to let Andy forget it. Easy-going Sauks didn't care much one way or another.

I dumped Andy unceremoniously in my bedroom and shut the door. The room has one tiny window that lets in precious little light during the day. At night, one's eyes never adjust to the dark. But it is private, so I was privileged. Susan and Ariel and Anthony had the two beds in a common room in the walk-out part of the basement.

Idaway is a classic Minnesota cabin, of which there are more than 120,000 in the state. It was built by my brother's father-in-law, who happened to be the pastor of the Salem Lutheran Church in our Nebraska hometown. Pastor Johnson purchased the lot with a seminary classmate. They chose well as it faces due west, providing many a spectacular sunset.

Early in the game, Pastor Johnson bought out his partner. He then proceeded to build Idaway in in stages. My sister-in-law, Cindy, remembers the first year they had indoor plumbing, the summer a toilet was installed, the year a living room with a fireplace was added on the south side of the cabin.

Pastor Johnson's five children eagerly anticipated their summer vacations at Idaway, when much of this work was done. They anticipated leaving Nebraska for the lakes of Minnesota much the way my siblings and I held our breath until August when our old Oldsmobile was packed up and we escaped the state.

While we prayed for rain all summer so we could get further than South Dakota, the Johnson kids had to hope no one in their father's Nebraska congregation died. His obligation to conduct a funeral often cut their holiday short. For many years the cabin didn't have a phone, so the grim news summoning them back to Nebraska was delivered by a neighbor. The sight of this woman making her way through the woods put the kids into a panic, with one of them sure to exclaim aloud, "Oh no, here comes Mrs. Ullven. Someone has died!"

Pastor Johnson and his wife retired in this cabin, but he passed away just a few years later. Since the snows are deep and the winters long in Minnesota, his widow did not want to live there alone. So, Charlie bought the cabin in a fifty-fifty partnership with Cindy's brother.

"It still says Johnson's Idaway, with no mention of the Leonard connection," I once remarked. "Now that your part-owner, shouldn't your name be on it as well?"

"No," Charlie said. "It will always be the Johnson cabin. That's the way it should be."

Having been raised by three sisters, my brother has a feminist side.

Not that he hasn't left his mark on the property. Over the years, Charlie has added an expansive deck and a screened-in porch. The cabin is built into a steep hillside, so the lake-view deck is at treetop level. The screened porch, which sits on the north side of the house, is a lovely respite from the ravenous Minnesota mosquitoes. It was also a perfect birdwatching retreat for Sauks and Andy.

Mike and I made several summer escapes from Houston to Idaway. The first time, he complained bitterly the entire drive. We'd arrived in Minneapolis mid-afternoon on a Thursday and the long-weekend cabin traffic up I-94 was terrible.

"Tell me again why we're doing this?" Mike grumbled as traffic ground to dead stop for no apparent reason. "What was wrong with Minneapolis?"

"Trust me, you'll see when we get there," I assured him.

In the tradition begun by Pastor Johnson, Charlie had been working at the cabin on a weeklong vacation. Assisting him with a multitude of projects were his son, Chris, and a nephew on Cindy's side. Mike and I walked in just as Charlie put out an evening meal of brats and beans and onions.

Mike grinned and elbowed me. "What do you see?"

"Uh, dinner?"

"Man food. The only green thing on the table is pickles. I love it!"

Mike and I made several more trips to Lake Ida in the coming years. To say it is an improvement over Houston in the summer is a vast understatement. But when I arrived in mid-August 2016, I did not yet comprehend how long the hours can get in even one of the most ideal settings.

Chapter 24: Cabin fever

August 12 through August 21, with a one-night respite

Even voluntary retirement can be disconcerting, or so more and more of my friends and acquaintances tell me.

Therefore, I suppose it is no small wonder that the unexpected end of my career changed me in ways I couldn't have begun to imagine. A case in point is my lowered threshold for boredom. For all my adult years, I'd only had so much time to devote to my personal life, be it traveling, catching up with friends and family, or writing. Suddenly, I had vast stretches of time with nothing scheduled and just about nothing that absolutely needed to be done at any given point in time.

I found myself profoundly bored but without the discipline to undertake all the things I'd longed to do while working. I became a master at procrastination. I kept thinking about several of my friends who had been supported by their husbands for decades. I hated it when a task I could accomplish on the way to work not only took them a full day, but stressed them out besides. I always swore I wouldn't become like them, and now I was running the risk of doing precisely that, albeit with self-awareness rather than the woe-is-me bitching I'd hear when their routine of mostly leisure and pleasure was interrupted.

I also gained a new perspective on my final years with Mike, especially the last few trips we made together. As days at Idaway stretched away ahead of me with no end in sight, I particularly reflected on our trip to Argentina in November 2008.

I was covering a convention in Mar del Plata, a seaside resort about 200 miles southeast of Buenos Aires, while simultaneously putting out the weekly newsletter I co-edited. In other words, it was a typical, double-duty business trip with a bit of jet lag thrown in for good measure.

And I wasn't going all the way to Argentina without doing some sightseeing. Why else would Mike be with me? While's Mike's presence often solicited some consternation from one co-worker or another, I maintained this was bullshit. Not only did he strictly pay his way, but he always acted as my personal assistant, making my business trips easier.

Buenos Aires, where we arrived a few days before the conference, proved to be such a case. While I worked in the hotel, Mike spent an entire day trying first one and then another option for getting us down to the coast. The trains were booked months in advance, a driver was too expensive, and we didn't want to rent a car. In retrospect, it would have far easier to drive in Argentina than in Italy, which I've done on multiple occasions.

Mike reported each of these setbacks as he'd once again return to the hotel to announce defeat while I was filing stories sitting cross-legged on the bed as our tiny hotel room did not have a desk.

"I'm going to the bus station," he said, "it's our last option.

And indeed it was. We made our way by bus, a dusty journey in a well-worn and not very clean vehicle memorable mostly for the toilet that simply opened onto the pavement below.

Once in Mar del Plata, I was horrified to discover that unlike other South American conferences I had attended, this one provided no English translation. If I didn't file a comprehensive story on the event, there would be hell to pay. At a minimum, the company would probably refuse to cover my expenses. Termination was unlikely, but there would no doubt be painful recriminations. Not to put too fine a point on it, but an oil man can often get away unscathed by pleading innocence or ignorance while a woman in the industry will be held accountable for an act of God.

In the end, a co-worker whose Spanish is much better than mine—but then whose isn't, as my skills are pretty much limited to ordering a beer and finding the bathroom—clued me in to the gist of a presentation.

With this meager information plus conference materials that included a paper written in English, I cobbled something together and filed it while listening to Obama's victory speech in my hotel room. The article was far from my best work, but it would serve to keep me employed.

Our final four days in Argentina were spent at an estancia. I was exhausted and anticipated relaxing in a lovely hacienda. And it was lovely: wide verandas draped in blooming jasmine; an elegant bedroom furnished with antiques; beautifully tended grounds in the midst of a eucalyptus grove; fragrant, flowering citrus trees; a private swimming pool; and an entire household staff at our disposal, that is if we could make our requests understood as they did not speak a word of English.

I was in heaven, but Mike was in hell. While I was catching my breath from an exhausting business trip, Mike was bored out of his mind.

"We traveled how many thousands of miles so you could vacation in Nebraska?" he complained to the accompaniment of lowing cattle.

Mike had a point. While it was certainly prettier than Nebraska, it had just about the same number of entertainment options. Mike and I argued until we ran out of words and then just ignored each other. Even at the time, I knew I was being unfair to Mike. He had not worked for more than three years. His threshold for boredom was much lower than mine.

I've often thought of that Argentina trip since I was laid off, but never more than the week and a half I spent at Idaway in August 2016.

The lake was beautiful and the weather divine. I could swim in crystal clear open water to my heart's content. I could write for hours on end. I could delve into that pile of books I'd been meaning to read. I could go on long bike rides. And yet I was bored to tears.

Each morning I'd wake up in the crypt and wonder when I would be able to escape.

And that was the problem. I was in a holding pattern over which I had no control. With obligations back in Arkansas, Susan, Ariel, and Anthony had left after a long weekend. Charlie was supposed to be on a weeklong vacation but, like Pastor Johnson before him, had been called back to his parish a couple hundred miles away to conduct a funeral.

So, it came down to Cindy and me. She was gainfully employed and yearned for the downtime. I could vaguely remember what that was like. Meanwhile, I was reliving Mike's experience in Argentina.

My brother and sister-in-law were far too accommodating in that extraordinary "Minnesota Nice" way. Since Andy and Ted couldn't get along, they'd gone so far as to cut Ted's vacation short.

195

Charlie packed him up for the return trip to his home in Blooming Prairie, a small town about an hour's drive south of the Twin Cities.

Now Sauks and Andy had full run of the cabin. They spent much of their time napping on the screened porch. Cindy politely turned a blind eye when Sauks decided to put a few marks of his own on a well-worn cabin sofa. In other words, they were ungrateful little shits.

I strived to be a better houseguest than the cats, but that isn't much of a challenge since I don't scar furniture or pick fights with my guests' pets. I was beginning to get a bit homesick for Houston, which in August was beyond absurd. I could have just moved on but didn't want to miss my niece. Charlie's daughter, Karin, and her husband Steve were on vacation in the Montana Rockies, well out of cell phone range. No one was quite sure when they would return.

Another thing I learned about myself during the summer of 2016 is I need to be within striking distance of a substantial urban area. I've known from the time I left Nebraska in my rearview mirror I wasn't going back there, but I've long dreamed of retiring in a scenic, rural place.

Scrap that. After living first in the Denver area and then on the fringes of Houston, I am too accustomed to a multitude of good restaurants, shopping venues, and cultural events at my fingertips, in addition to a good-sized airport.

In this regard, Tijeras was perfect. I could hike into the national forest from my front door, but Albuquerque was just a ten-minute drive down the mountain. And all the artistic and cuisine offerings of Santa Fe were a scenic one-hour drive up the Turquoise Trail. The Albuquerque airport was small but adequate, offering multiple, daily non-stop flights to Houston, from which I can fly just about anywhere.

Don't get me wrong. Alexandria is a far cry from Wayne, Nebraska. This western Minnesota town has a population pushing 12,000 and, with all the lakes in the area and its location right off I-94, it attracts its fair share of visitors. Therefore, Alex—as it is known locally— has a large, well-stocked grocery store and several adequate dining options. But it's still too small and quiet for me.

Fortunately, the Arkansas clan had no sooner left when Cindy and I received an invitation to the Twin Cities. Charlie and Cindy's son, Chris, who had graduated from the University of Minnesota med school a couple months earlier, happened to have a short break from his residency. We were set for an overnight stay in the big city. So, on Wednesday, August 17, Cindy and I left Sauks and Andy to inflict whatever damage they might to the cabin, and made a two-hour trip down I-94 to the St. Paul suburb of Roseville.

I cannot say enough positive things about Minneapolis-St. Paul. I've never had anything but a lovely time there. Now that I am retired, people ask all the time: Anne, will you leave Texas to be with family?

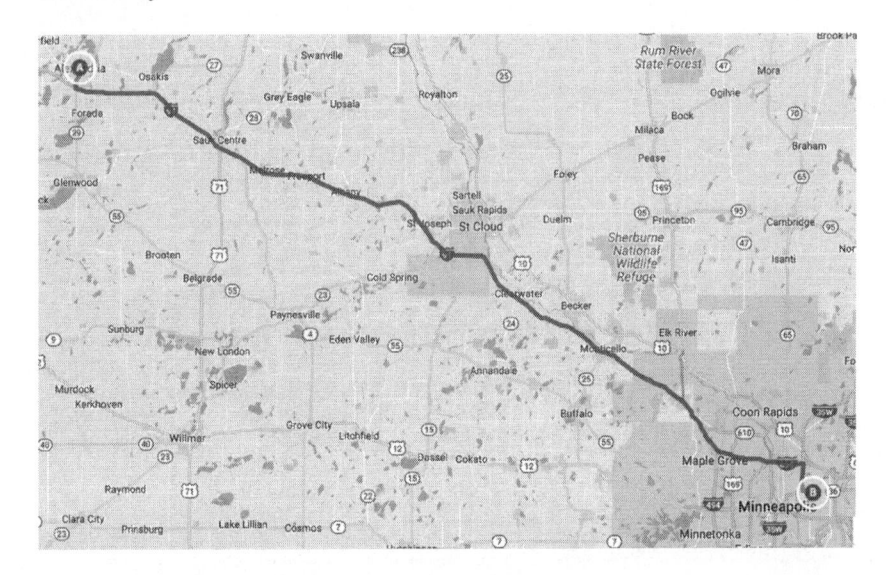

The answer never varies: Colorado is too expensive and they hate Texans; Arkansas is as hot as Texas most of the time; and Minnesota, well Minnesota not only has winter but arguably the most brutal winter in the lower forty-eight.

Otherwise, the Twin Cities might be a consideration: a major metropolis (sixteenth in the U.S.), progressive politics that make it one of the most liberal cities in the country, cutting-edge dining scene, beautiful setting, wonderful park system, friendly people, and a major airport.

What isn't to love? Again, it can be summed up in one word: winter.

When Mike and I were sheltering from the brutal heat and humidity of a Houston July, we would often console ourselves by watching the Coen brothers' *Fargo*. In the scene where William Macy gets out of his car to angrily chip the ice off his windshield, we'd turn to each other and say, "yes, there is a reason we put up with this shit."

"A Pizza Luce nearby makes just about anywhere livable."

Okay, I'd already had a couple glasses of wine when my nephew showed up at the Pizza Luce a few miles from his Roseville townhouse, so I can't swear to the exact veracity of this quote. But Chris said something to this effect and I couldn't have agreed more.

The food and wine at Pizza Luce were delightful. After just a couple days in Alexandria (okay, I was in Nebraska and Wyoming before that), every specialty pizza on the menu looked better than the last. And this observation was made while fondly reminiscing about the pizzas I've had in Europe.

I grew up, needless to say, on a Nebraska version of pizza. It was heavy on meat, cheese, and dough. If made right, it can be amazingly good while bearing little or no resemblance to its old-world ancestor. I had one in an Iowa bar some years back that I still dream about, and if you haven't caught on yet: I can be a food snob.

Pizza Luce, in contrast, offered lots of fresh basil and garlic, arugula, and a wide variety of mushrooms and smoked Italian meats. I could almost taste the ultra-thin and crispy pizzas topped with arugula and prosciutto, zucchini, or melanzane (eggplant) that were a staple of my diet those two summers in Geneva. If you're wondering, "What? Pizza in Switzerland?" let me point out that Geneva is within sixty miles of the Italian border.

After indulging in pizza and more wine al fresco in the Minnesota twilight, we went to Chris and his wife Barb's townhouse. I was pleased to see the Stratocaster I'd given Chris in that bittersweet summer after Mike died on display.

Mike owned a number of beautiful guitars, both electric and acoustic, but the Stratocaster was the one I'd find lying on the sofa—along with an ashtray full of butts—when I got up early to go to work in our final months together. It would be only two or three hours after Mike had finally crawled in bed beside me.

The ashtray says you've been up all night.

Those Wilco lyrics continue to haunt me. Mike must have known he was very ill but refused to find out what was wrong.

Therefore, the Stratocaster was the guitar I was painfully sentimental about and the one I wanted to stay in my family.

In addition to the pleasure of the seeing the Stratocaster, I was treated to the company of Chris and Barb's two cats, Karl Malone and Sonny (as in Sonny Boy Williamson). Cats named after an NBA star and a legendary blues musician? Well, why not? And, have there ever been two more opposite cats living together than Karl and Sonny? Karl is the epitome of an asshole cat, the snarky, fuck-you, swatting demon that only the most dedicated cat people can love. On the other hand, Sonny is—pardon the pun—just that, a warm, fuzzy, friendly feline as golden as a summer sunset. But it's Karl Malone's portrait that is displayed next to the Stratocaster. And he is so attached to his owner he apparently had a mental breakdown the week Chris and Barb married.

Weddings can be tough on all participants. Multiple parties, occasionally including the bride, want everything to be just so. There's always too much to do in too little time with conflicting opinions on how these things can best be accomplished.

People often lose control or behave badly. I know of what I speak as I closed a heavy door on Don's head at Marcia's wedding. It was purely an accident. I didn't know he was following me as I huffed out of a room in a rage, but the resulting bloody wound and sympathy bestowed upon Don for having such a bitch of a wife was not amongst my finer moments.

Karl Malone spent the week of Chris and Barb's wedding in the main bedroom of Idaway, located directly above the crypt. I ventured in once or twice to say hello, at which point he hissed and promptly darted under the bed.

Shortly after the big event, Karl became very ill. Good thing Chris and Barb had put off their honeymoon as an emergency trip to the vet was in order. It seems, in the stress of the nuptials, Karl had swallowed a penny.

One of the things cats have over dogs on the evolutionary scale is the sense not to eat anything and everything put in front of them. This includes not only an aversion to non-food items like tennis balls and shoes, but also an inherent sense of what flora or fauna are poisonous.

So how Karl managed to swallow a penny is anyone's guess. Intentional suicide? Thankfully, while he was one ailing kitty both before and after surgery, he has fully recovered to torment all humans around him for another day.

Pastor Charlie returned to Idaway on Sunday, August 21. His vacation was shot and he was exhausted. To top it off, he had a job interview in the Twin Cities the next day. Karin and Steve were still off the grid in Montana somewhere. Chris? Well he had taken some of his very few spare minutes to spend with his mother and me the previous week, so I didn't want to impose upon him again.

So, as if I weren't already an inconvenience to everyone I knew in the Land of 10,000 Lakes, I now had nowhere to go. I could have headed south toward home, but still wanted to see Karin and Steve. I scratched my head, looked at the cats, and thought: Well, I've never been to Northfield. I'd heard it is nice and I was a big fan of *The Long Riders* back in the day. And so, I decided to give the town where most of the Jesse James gang met its fate a try.

Using my hotspot – which I'd been trying to refrain from doing while at the cabin for fear of an astronomical phone bill – I searched for lodging in Northfield and was surprised to see The Archer House took pets. Karin had worked at this historical hotel one summer while in college.

I called to make sure they took pets. It took two tries before a sleepy-sounding receptionist picked up. I asked for a pet room and gave her my credit card number. The critters and I were set—or so I thought.

Chapter 25: Hotel hell

August 22: Alexandria to Northfield, 174 miles

Every holiday has its low point. Since I've traveled so much, I know the symptoms well, an overwhelmingly blue feeling of what am I doing here and why am I not home? I take it as a temporary bout of homesickness that even a seasoned traveler like me is subject to.

Like vertigo, when and where it happens is unpredictable. Sometimes it is caused by an all-too-common travel travail like a missed connection or a booking in what turns out to be crummy hotel in an even crummier neighborhood. Other times it can be attributed to nothing at all. On a road trip across Switzerland it hit my two co-travelers and me simultaneously. Everyone save our gracious host was grumpy and out of sorts. It was a beautiful, sunny day in early October. Lake Lucerne was a bright blue gem fringed with golden trees set against a backdrop of snow-capped Alps. We were in one of the planet's garden spots, so why for Christ sake were we all so damn pissy?

For me in the summer of 2016, it happened during my trip to Northfield. And it was caused by numerous factors: Nearly a week and a half of cabin ennui followed by Monday's slow-and-go crawl around the southwestern quadrant of the Twin Cities in rush-hour traffic, topped off by a ridiculous hotel policy administered by a surly twenty-something.

My spirits rose upon turning down Northfield's historic Division Street, which parallels the Cannon River and is lined with charming shops and restaurants. I am a history buff, and I could now chalk up seeing another iconic site in American history annals. The town's armed resistance of Jesse James's attempted bank robbery in September 1876 has even been called the final battle of the Civil War, since the James-Younger Gang was part of a post-war insurgency.

I found a parking place and walked into The Archer House anticipating a very pleasant evening. That high evaporated when the desk clerk—who at no point could be bothered to even smile—informed me the hotel allows dogs but not cats.

I got absolutely nowhere by pointing out that: one, no one told me this when I'd booked a pet room the night before; and two, a cat would forgo elimination rather than pee or poop on the floor. Neither did my lie that the cats are declawed, which of course they aren't.

"Let me speak to your manager then."

"He's not here."

"Then call him."

Rather than use the phone by her hand, she glumly walked about ten paces back to where she'd been sitting when I'd arrived. When she got the manager on that phone, I was not particularly surprised that she did not signal for me to come over. Nonetheless, it pissed me off. I listened with a clenched jaw as she indulged in a lengthy, hushed conversation. From what I could gather from my end, their concern was not what to do with the unhappy customer in their lobby but rather which employee to blame.

This went on for about ten excruciating minutes as my blood pressure continued to percolate. Then she hung up and came back to the front desk.

I waited for her to say something. Anything.

Without a word or even a glance, she began surfing the computer. With more restraint than I thought I had, I didn't break the silence until she picked up the phone she'd pointedly not used to call the manager.

"Who are you calling?" I asked.

"A kennel where you can board your cats."

"And you were going to ask me when? Never mind that I asked to speak to your manager, a request which you chose to ignore." My voice was shrill. There's nothing I hate more than when someone finally grinds me down to the point of high-pitched anger.

The final insult came when I pointed out that they'd already run my credit card.

"Well, duh," this young woman said, "you're not staying here so we'll just tear it up."

I did not insert the "duh" with literary license. She really said it.

I salvaged what I could out of the evening (and my ever diminishing self worth) with the guaranteed endorphin booster of hot curry. And while the AmericInn was not on a charming downtown street within walking distance of bars and restaurants, but rather on a main highway with a view of huge grain elevators, the staff was friendly and my room was well appointed and—best of all given my last two weeks—above ground.

Chapter 26: Still singing the blues

August 23: Northfield, Minnesota, to Nerstrand Big Woods State Park (12 miles) to Mantorville (30 miles) to Blooming Prairie (28 miles), for a total of 75 miles.

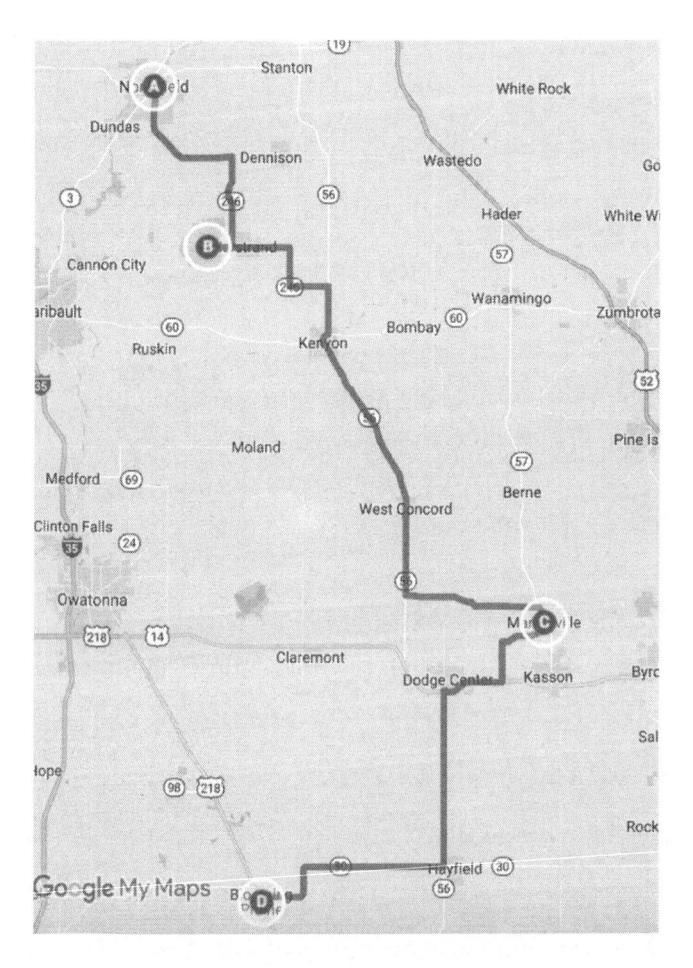

Despite the excellent curry and very comfortable bed well above ground (as opposed to the crypt back at Idaway), I woke up the next morning in a funk. I was still in Minnesota and still at loose ends. I wasn't even sure where I was going to spend the night, although I now knew Karin and Steve were on their way back to the Twin Cities. Perhaps I'd head that way.

One way or another, I figured I'd had enough of Northfield, or maybe it was Northfield had had enough of my grumpy ass and furry co-travelers.

So, I packed up and headed to Nerstrand-Big Woods. A hike usually turns my mood around and some tourist literature in the lobby mentioned this state park just twelve miles to the south-southeast. Its name indicated there'd be plenty of shade and therefore Sauks and Andy would be fine in the car.

True to its name, Nerstrand is a nearly pristine remnant of the temperate hardwood forest known as the Big Woods that once covered much of south-central Minnesota and western Wisconsin. Translated directly from the French Grand Bois, if Big Woods brings to mind the first of Laura Ingalls Wilder's *Little House* books, you have hit the nail on the head.

Little House in the Big Woods is set outside of Pepin, about sixty miles to the east in western Wisconsin. My brother Charlie (not to be confused with Laura's father, Charles Ingalls) raised his family in Menomonie, Wisconsin, just a few dozen miles north of Pepin. Once when all branches of our immediate family gathered in Menomonie for a reunion, Karin—just old enough to drive—took us to the Laura Ingalls Wilder birthplace. While the *Little House* has been faithfully reconstructed, my younger niece from Colorado was more than a bit distraught to see no woods whatsoever.

That's because they were all cut down by the lumber barons, one of which founded Menomonie. Nerstrand was saved from this fate as small, sustainable woodlots were divided up between the early settlers in the 1850s in the manner of their European homeland. Because of the multiple land owners, subsequent lumber barons were thwarted in their attempts to harvest this last stand. Ironically, I was listening to an audio of Annie Proulx's *Barkskins*—an epic novel set against the backdrop of the deforestation of North America—when I turned off Minnesota Highway 146 into Nerstrand-Big Woods.

As I'd guessed, the park provided more than enough cover for Sauks and Andy to nap in a cool car while I walked three or four miles on undulating trails through thick stands of elm, maple, and oak. It was green and cool and lovely, but I still missed the wide vistas of the west and its heart-thumping climbs at higher altitudes.

I wasn't even sure where my next stop was going to be until I got a call from Charlie to meet him for lunch in Mantorville.

"Manor Ville?" I asked.

He spelled it out for me and my GPS told me it was thirty miles to the south-southeast. I took several ninety-degree turns through tall corn fields sectioned off into one-mile squares that equal 640 acres. Farmland, no matter how lush, does not generally inspire me, but I did find it mildly interesting that the farms were much grander than the ones back in northeastern Nebraska.

As I dipped down into a town of quaint, golden-hued limestone buildings, I suddenly felt transported somewhere far from Minnesota. Mantorville is one of the oldest towns in the state and its namesake limestone was quarried nearby. It felt oddly familiar because of the multiple business trips I've made to the Cotswolds west of London, an area also known for its buttery limestone architecture.

Charlie and I met at the Hubbell House.

"Your cats in the car?" he asked.

"Where else?" I shrugged, pointing at the Honda down the street. "They should be okay for an hour or so."

Constructed in 1856, the Hubbell House features an impressive list of guests going back more than a century. Over my second good meal in a row, Charlie informed me—in that delicate, cautious Minnesota manner—that I was welcome to spend the night with him and Cindy in Blooming Prairie, but my beasts were to be confined to the basement.

"Fair enough," I assured him. I followed him another twenty-eight miles southward to Blooming Prairie.

Blooming Prairie is the second small town my brother has lived in since his mid-life career change. Following his ordination in 2004, he was first assigned to a church in Montevideo, a town of some 5,000 in southwestern Minnesota. Blooming Prairie only has about 2,000 people, but doesn't feel quite as remote since it is closer to the Twin Cities as well as Rochester, home of the renowned Mayo Clinic.

"Where's Ted?" I asked as we made our way down Charlie's steep basement steps. Andy was a black furry bowling ball in my arms, while Charlie was carrying the calmer, better-behaved Sauks.

"Upstairs on our bed. He won't come down."

Never say never. Before we could close the door behind us, a streak of brown tabby fur flew by. Andy catapulted out of my arms. Ted, Andy, and I chased each other around the various corners of the basement several times before the cats screeched to a snarling, growling, hissing halt by the massive furnace.

So much for keeping the peace in Blooming Prairie. Charlie grabbed Ted while I held Andy back, apologizing profusely.

It seems every cat I've owned has a trait shared by no other. With Murphy it was her love of the plastic rings that seal milk cartons. For years after her passing, I'd find one squirreled away in a sofa cushion or under a piece of heavy furniture.

Fig was the only cat who would come running when I turned on the television, knowing I'd sit still long enough for her to snuggle in my armpit. If Don and I didn't get up early enough to please Arthur, he'd swat at the door stop to generate a good, annoying "sprong."

Andy has several unique traits, including his willingness to sit on my lap while I'm outdoors. Granted I have to hold on fairly tightly to let him know he's not going any further, but he is generally cooperative enough that I can enjoy a cup of coffee or glass of wine al fresco with him.

Since Andy stood at the top of the basement steps attempting to wear us down with his persistent, Siamese-pitched cries, I spent much of my evening in Blooming Prairie doing precisely that. Sauks, on the other hand, was happily exploring the thousand nooks and crannies of Charlie and Cindy's extraordinarily well-organized basement.

Chapter 27: Back to civilization

August 24: Blooming Prairie to Richfield: 77 miles

There was no trick to getting Andy into the car the next morning. He was at the top of the basement steps at the first sound of activity in the kitchen. I scooped him up and deposited him in a carrier while I was still packing the car. Otherwise, it was just a matter of time before he'd figure out what was going on and take cover.

Which was precisely what Sauks did. He'd been more than content in the basement and upon Andy's capture, quickly hid. I didn't know where to even begin to look.

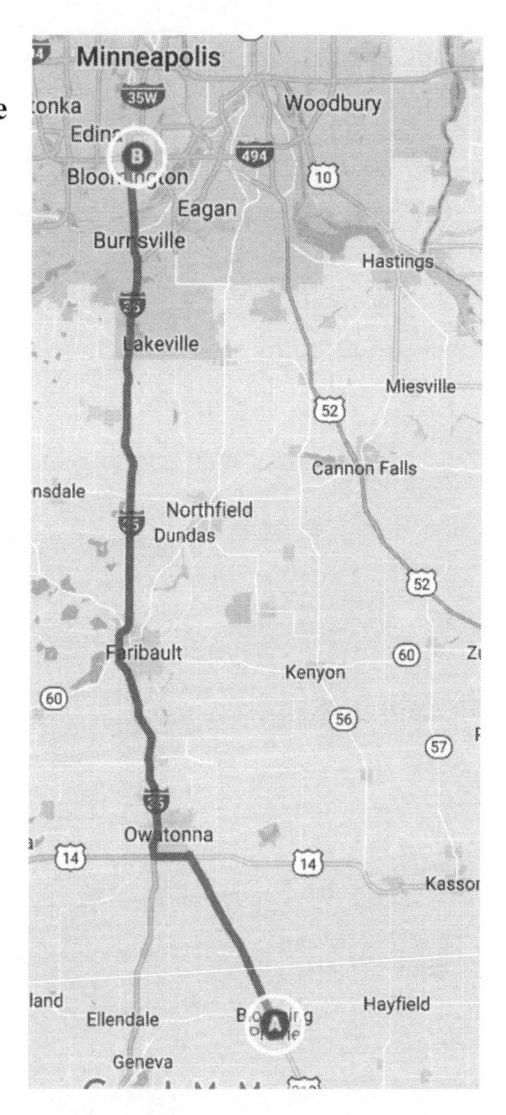

"You may be stuck with us," I said resignedly to Cindy.

I'd returned up to the kitchen to pour myself another cup of coffee in hopes of getting Sauks to let his guard down.

"Let me try," she said. Cindy went down the steps while I hovered near the top out of view.

"Sauks," she called out in her best soft, Minnesota-accented healing voice (she is an RN at the Mayo clinic). I didn't witness it, but he popped his head out of a box of Christmas decorations to be petted. If it hadn't been for Cindy, he'd probably still be down there.

By now, I had been on the road for over three weeks, and was still more than a week and a half and one thousand miles from home. My car was a disaster. I had no idea what clothes and toiletries were where, and the cats and I had left a trail of havoc in our wake. Figuring all three of us needed a respite, I'd booked a room for that night at the Candlewood Suites near the Minneapolis-St. Paul airport, only a few miles from where Karin and Steve live.

Karin, who is a fiddler in a blue grass band, had a gig that night, so she and her husband had ventured out of the Montana woods the day before. I knew I could snag an invite to her show and was excited about it. After weeks of small towns, I was going out in the big city.

Everything in travel is relative. How else to explain how happy I was in a hotel nestled between big box stores and car dealerships just off I-494? My cats and I were not going to be a hassle to anyone but ourselves.

As I made multiple trips up and down the hallway, taking just about everything out of my car, I was serenaded by a dog behind nearly every door. Candlewood is indeed pet friendly and God bless them for that.

Sauks and Andy were happy too. Our single window offered a view of one scrawny tree and the Mitsubishi dealership next door, but to a cat, a window is a window.

I took everything out of my two suitcases, sorted clothes, collected huge piles of laundry, and anticipated wearing something different from the same handful of items I'd made do over the last three weeks.

It was heaven.

"Why are you staying here? Please come and stay with us."

Such was Karin's greeting as they picked me up for an evening with the Potluck String Band.

"Oh, Sauks and Andy are so badly behaved. I can't impose them upon you, let alone Tibby."

Tibby is Karin and Steve's cat. Another brown tabby, he'd hung out with Ted periodically until they decided they couldn't stand each other. Such is life in a cat's social world.

"They can stay in the guest room. It will be fine."

Karin made it her litany over the next two days, which was just the time it took for Sauks, Andy, and me to regain our wits in the solitude of the Candlewood. On Friday, we moved the few miles down I-494 to Karin and Steve's.

But first I was off to The Amsterdam Pub in St. Paul. I ate a huge pot of mussels to the accompaniment of the Potluck String Band, had an interesting conversation or two, and was thrilled to be back in civilization.

Chapter 28: Minnesota living

Bloomington, August 25 through August 29

"I'm bringing Sauks and Andy over," I texted Karin, "before they have a chance to hide. Then I'll come back and pack up."

I put my iPhone down to do just that, and found both had disappeared.

How did they know? I've owned cats for so long and had been on the road enough with these two to not waste time wondering.

So much for Plan A. Since they were both now huddled under the recliner, I went to Plan B and packed up everything else before burrowing under the chair to grab their furry little asses

"Are you from Arkansas?"

The young man in front of me in the sangria line at the Minnesota State Fair was wearing a Fayettechill tee shirt.

"Yes. How did you know?"

"Your shirt." Ariel and Anthony had given me one with the same logo. "I have family in Fayetteville. In fact, I'm heading down there day after tomorrow. Are you visiting?"

"No, I just moved here. Got a job after graduation. I love it."

Hard to argue with that. We were perfectly comfortable outdoors on a bright, sunny day in August. For southerners, this is nothing short of a miracle. I resisted saying, "Just wait until January and see if you feel the same way."

Still it was warm enough to warrant several glasses of sangria. How one can get drunk on sangria is something of a mystery, and yet that is precisely what happened. The encounter with the Fayettechill tee shirt is one of my few non-fuzzy memories of the day.

Under normal circumstances, I would have resisted a visit to a state fair like the plague. In fact, despite being the resident of several different states, the only other state fair I'd been to before was the Nebraska's in Lincoln, once with my parents when I was a kid and then again on a date in college. It was during the second visit that I learned that beer and carnival rides don't mix. I kept everything down that evening, but had the dry heaves for hours the following day. Haven't been on anything more daunting than a Ferris wheel since.

Karin is a braver soul than me. At the end of a long day, she and a friend got on one of the most stomach-churning rides of all. And I believe she matched me sangria for sangria. She also managed to expertly fiddle her way through a set with the Potluck String Band. But then, she is young.

I give high marks to the Minnesota State Fair. There was the usual excess of fried food, but then who knew olives stuffed with blue cheese and deep-fat fried on a stick were so damn good? And the exhibit halls were fascinating, or at least what I remember of them.

The Twin Cities are heaven in August. That's the main reason I'd made Karin and Steve's my refuge the summer of 2009, just five months after Mike died. It had been my first time in their house, which is tucked into a deep, narrow valley just off I-494. It was such a sad summer, even walks through the woods at the end of their street and around nearby Mount Normandale Lake—with its backdrop of a hulking seventy-meter ski jump—did little to ease my pain.

Now, the cats and I were happily ensconced in the basement guest room, which has a much larger window than the crypt. Since it opens at ground level, it provided a perfect perch for Andy and Sauks to window hunt for birds and squirrels.

Tibby spent much of his day just outside our room. The cats might have gotten along. Once I forgot to shut my door and both Andy and Sauks began to explore the basement without any immediate Tibby repercussions. But after the two Ted incidents, I was more than happy to keep them separate. After all, it was Tibby's house.

The suburb of Bloomington is located north of the Minnesota River, just before its confluence with the Mississippi. It is quite scenic with numerous lakes nestled among wooded hills.

Nephew Chris told me that for some reason Bloomington's bucolic parks attract suicidal men prone to shooting their brains out on the shore of one of its numerous lakes at sunrise.

"Can you imagine," he asked, "the happy morning jogger that comes upon that sight?"

Chris has a dark sense of humor that is no doubt an asset in a career in medicine.

A quick Internet check brings up a suicide cleanup service in Bloomington. Is this normal? I didn't find one for Sugar Land, so it seems Chris may be on to something.

That Internet search informed me that Bloomington's Mall of America is also a hot spot for suicides. I had ventured into this behemoth a couple times, albeit never willingly as I have something of an aversion to malls and can only shake my head at people who find them entertaining. I worked for years across the street from Houston's Galleria. Some of my co-workers loved spending their lunch hours over there, while it took an act of will for me to enter the doors long enough to grab some fast food.

In 1985, the Metropolitan Stadium—which had been the home of the Minnesota Vikings—was razed to make room for the Mall of America. Bloomington first crossed my radar screen during Viking games when I was a child. Northeast Nebraska is Scandinavian enough there were plenty of Viking fans around. I recall being puzzled—Bloomington? Where's Bloomington?—until some adult explained it was a Minneapolis suburb.

I'd left New Mexico in great physical shape. I hiked at least once a day, and often twice, which was good for both body and soul. I made the lung-busting three-mile-plus climb up to Sandia Crest by way of Tree Spring Trail several times. On the days when temperatures crept into the nineties, leaving me a bit housebound, I'd drive up to Tecolote (Spanish for owl) Trail. This three-mile loop at nearly 9,000 feet offered shade, breezes, and temperatures at least ten degrees cooler.

Therefore, I was in good enough form to hike up to Pitkin Lake on my trip to Vail in July.

"Anne will never make it," my brother-in-law John had declared over dinner the night before.

Well, that gave me the determination to do just that. The in-and-out trek of nearly nine miles takes one up above tree line at 11,362 feet with an elevation gain of nearly 3,000 feet. I huffed and puffed and was the last one up to the lake, but by God, I made it.

Alas, since leaving New Mexico, I'd gotten precious little exercise. This was particularly shameful while I was at Idaway with nothing better to do. And yet, I'd only gotten on my bike several times while there.

I'd hauled that mountain bike up to New Mexico, only to be too intimidated by the true mountain bikers I had encountered while hiking to ever get on it in that mountainous terrain.

So, when Karin suggested we bike to Eden Prairie to her favorite coffee shop I was game.

Minneapolis-St. Paul has a network of bike trails places like Houston could only dream about. Just two or three blocks of our seven-mile ride was on city streets, and quiet ones at that.

Karin is a fellow author and the coffee shop in the historic Smith Douglas More House is one of her favorite writing retreats.

This red-brick farm house, which was built in 1877, is one of the last remaining historical buildings in Eden Prairie. The local historical society decided a coffee shop would bring in more people than a museum. Beyond the entrance, where the coffee is brewed and food, beer, and wine are served, the house remains authentic, down to stained glass windows and creaking floorboards.

We drank a glass of wine under the arbor before riding the seven miles back on an alternate route. I made it further than Karin up one long, steep hill, before surrendering to gravity. Karin was impressed. I attributed it to the time I'd spent in the mountains, but was secretly ashamed I'd not made it to the top.

Chapter 29: One long-ass day

August 30: Bloomington, Minnesota, to Rogers, Arkansas: 657 miles

The drive from Minneapolis to northwest Arkansas is not one of my favorites. In fact, I'd have a hard time coming up with a long-distance drive I dislike more. Generally, if part of a day's drive sucks, like say the northern part of Kansas if you're making your way between Houston and Wayne, Nebraska, another part of it is decent, like the Arbuckle Mountains in southern Oklahoma. Even the drive from northeastern Nebraska to Denver, one I had made countless times when living first in Nebraska and then Colorado, at least has a change or two in scenery, albeit not particularly inspiring ones until the Rockies appear as a dim blue line on the western horizon.

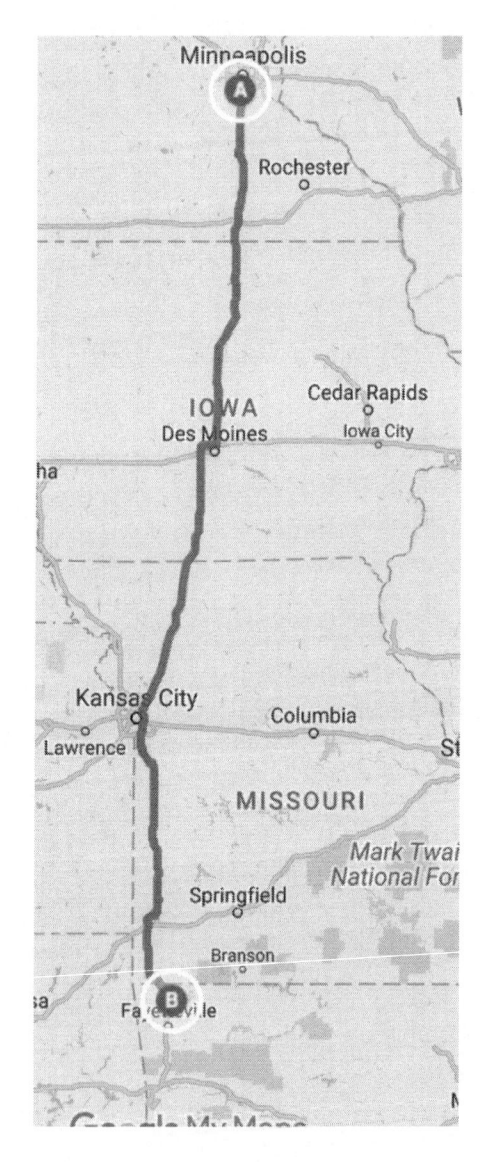

On the other hand, the drive on I-35 from Minneapolis to Kansas City and then down to the Arkansas state line on I-49 is comprised of mile after unrelenting mile of farmland. And in Iowa, all that farmland is planted in corn.

Another thing to detest about this drive is that once you've made it from top to bottom through Iowa, a distance of two hundred and twelve miles, you have to do it all over again in Missouri, which has the audacity to be a hundred miles longer.

But before beginning that boring trek, I first had to get out of Minnesota. I made no particular effort to hit the road early. One of the best things about being unemployed is not having to deal with rush-hour traffic. I took my time packing up and it was about nine when I said goodbye to Karin and headed south. I had nearly ten hours of driving ahead of me, but still hoped to make my destination before dark.

I hadn't even cleared the southernmost suburbs when I got a call from Charlie asking if I'd like to meet him for a cup of coffee in Owatonna.

Of course I would. Fortunately, Charlie's path and mine now cross on a fairly regular basis, though I still remember when we'd go for more than a year without seeing each other.

We pulled into the parking lot of a Perkins at the same time. There was no shade, but the temperature was in the low seventies so Sauks and Andy would be okay for a short while.

I grabbed a quick bite, knowing I wouldn't eat again until I reached my niece Sarah and her husband Martin's house that evening. I apologized to Charlie again for my cats' behavior and thanked him for being such a gracious host.

It was late morning when I crossed into Iowa. One hundred miles down, five hundred and fifty-seven to go.

If there's anything interesting to see in Iowa I suppose it's in Madison County, southwest of Des Moines. Interstate 35 skirts the county to the east and there are signs for exits to see the covered bridges made famous by Robert James Waller's *The Bridges of Madison County* and the subsequent Clint Eastwood movie adaptation, which was filmed in and around Winterset. Winterset is also where John Wayne was born Marion Robert Morrison in 1907. Neither the bridges nor John Wayne museum tempted me. As always seems to be the case when in this part of the country, I was in an extreme hurry.

Another disheartening thing about this drive is the frequency with which I make it. This would be my third time in 2016 alone. Susan and I had driven up for Chris's graduation in May, and it was on the return trip that I was hit with the gnawing premonition that my lover and I had hit the end of the road. This indeed proved to be the case as I got the dreaded call within days of my arrival back in Houston.

At Lamoni, I crossed into Missouri. This Iowa town of 2,000 is so close to the state line the first Anglo settlers in the area were slaveholders who thought they were indeed in Missouri.

If Lamoni sounds vaguely like an Old Testament prophet, it's because it was named after a king in the Book of Mormon. In 1870, Joseph Smith III formed this community for the Reorganized Church of Jesus Christ Latter Day Saints. To that end, the church's Graceland University is in located here.

My first husband Don was raised in this church. When I asked how it differed from the worldwide organization based in Salt Lake City, he didn't seem to know. It wasn't until years later that I read in Jon Krakauer's *Under the Banner of Heaven* that the break had been largely over the issue of polygamy. For obvious reasons, Joseph Smith's first wife did not approve of her husband's "God-given" directive to marry additional women. So, along with her oldest son, Joseph Smith III, and select others, she stayed behind and shunned the practice. Eventually, this group began their own church based on the Book of Mormon.

The church is now called the Community of Christ and they seem a bit more progressive than their Utah kin. For example, they allow the ordination of women clergy. If a "Mormon" sect ever comes to its senses and declares the Book of Mormon a bunch of early nineteenth century hooey, I'd bet on this one.

Missouri dragged on. A friend called to catch up as I made my way around the east side of Kansas City on I-494 in the early stages of rush hour traffic. We bantered back and forth for about a half an hour and I told him I was finally heading south and would see him soon.

Then it was the long, straight slog down I-49 toward Joplin. The late afternoon monotony was broken somewhat by a thundershower. To my surprise, the pounding rain and cracks of thunder solicited no response from either Sauks or Andy. Both were quieter than usual, as if the boring drive had lulled them into a stupor. I knew how they felt.

The sun had set by the time I finally drove into Bella Vista, Arkansas. The town's name and the fact that it was founded in 1965 as a resort community says it all. For the first time in more than six hundred miles the scenery had finally changed for the better. Located on a plateau in the Ozarks, Bella Vista has deep valleys, clear running streams, and steep rocky inclines, all of which I appreciated in the diminishing light.

I pulled up to Sarah and Martin's on Old White River Road about a half an hour later. It was now officially dark. Anthony came out to grab Sauks while I pried Andy out of the kitty condo. It was as if both cats had abandoned all hope of ever getting out of that car again.

Chapter 30: Almost home

August 31 through Sunday, September 4: Rogers, Arkansas

"Anne, your cat is out here waiting to be fed."

My nephew Matt didn't bother to knock as he opened my bedroom door and walked in holding Ivan in outstretched arms. He dumped the thin gray cat unceremoniously on the bed. Sauks, Andy, and I all jumped.

Of course, Ivan isn't my cat. He's Sarah's. But Sarah has her hands full with a directorship at Walmart Corporate and her son, Wallace, who was already well into his terrible twos despite the fact that today was his second birthday.

So, I've taken to pampering Ivan with Fancy Feast and a clean litter box when I'm visiting. Grateful for this attention, Ivan always remembers me. Even though it's often months between visits, he eagerly greets me at the door and then runs to his bowl indicating he knows who has the good cat food.

As was the case with Tibby, I think Sauks and Andy would have reached a peace agreement with Ivan. But Martin only tolerates Ivan's feline presence upon Sarah's insistence. He had made it clear he would grudgingly allow my cats under his roof only with the promise they not venture beyond my bedroom door.

Once again, Sauks, Andy, and I were holed up in a basement bedroom. Fortunately, this one, like Karin and Steve's, sported a large window that opens onto ground level. And by now, Andy and Sauks were conditioned to just appreciate not being in a car.

Sarah and Martin live on a cliff overlooking Beaver Lake, a fifty-mile reservoir with nearly five hundred miles of shoreline. Their eastern exposure provides some very nice sunrises if you're up early enough to witness them.

One of the reasons I'd long anticipated taking this trip is that not only does my far-flung family welcome me with open arms and put up with my unruly cats, they also offer me some very nice accommodations. While visiting I enjoy scenic views in the Vail Valley, at Lake Ida, and Rogers, Arkansas.

Of my three siblings and their families, I spend the most time with Susan's. Sarah is her oldest daughter, followed by Matt, who has been a best buddy of mine since we hiked together when he was a little boy, and last but hardly least, Ariel, who shares with me the initials A.E. I'm also quite close to respective husbands, Martin and Anthony.

Since I moved to a neighboring state when Sarah and Matt were small children and helped Susan and Jeff move when she was eight and a half months pregnant with Ariel, I am pretty much accepted as part of the inner circle.

This has its benefits and downsides. I have gone to bed alone and woken up with one of the gang sleeping next to me. "You don't snore as bad as Mom," Ariel told me on one such occasion. If I fail to lock my door, be it to the bathroom or the bedroom, I have automatically forfeited any privacy. And they often refer to me by the hated childhood nickname of Annabutt.

In other words, being in Rogers is as close to being at home as I can be without sleeping under my own roof.

With all the "privileges," there are often demands. Martin was finishing the last bit of renovation on their early 1970s-era home they had bought from the original owner. He was determined to have his man cave ready for Wallace's second birthday party that weekend.

So, I no sooner had arrived than a paint brush was thrust into my hand. Much of the next three days was spent on ladders, crouching at baseboards, and working my way around the built-in bar on my hands and knees painting. Good thing I like hard work. And it was not a solo effort, as Susan was also at it full time, and Sarah joined us when she could pawn Wallace off on her mother-in-law, who was also visiting.

On Thursday, Susan, Sarah, and I decided to take a break, if you can call lunch and a walk with a two-year-old a break.

We returned to an amusing sight. Martin's mother—who had thus far escaped painting duty—sat dejectedly on the floor, painting and pouting near the baseboards. With the main crew back on duty, she quickly tossed down her brush and retreated upstairs.

Wallace's birthday party on Saturday went by in a blur of gifts, wine, and cake. Regarding gifts, Susan gave him a painting Nancy had done called *The Monster in my House*. The monster is Marcus as boy is sitting in a corner, his shadow revealing a pair of horns.

Regarding the cake and wine, I was standing in the cake line with a glass of red in my hand when Anthony came up from behind and shoved a bit of heavily frosted cake up my nose. My wine went flying and of course I had on a white shirt.

Yes, Ariel's husband is an over-grown boy, or always the monster in the house.

By Sunday, we all felt like we deserved some down time. It was now September1, but that provides little or no relief as far south as Arkansas. Fortunately, the lake was at our feet and Martin has a boat.

We spent a lazy afternoon floating in one of Beaver Lake's countless coves. There was a cooler full of beer and wine, and good music blaring from the boat's sound system. Some of Martin's boat buddies joined us. Matt and Ariel swam to the shore to explore the limestone boulders and cliffs that line the lake while we watched.

Beaver Lake was created by the damming of the White River in the early 1960s. The White River is sourced in the Boston Mountains of northwest Arkansas, makes a short loop northward into southern Missouri, and then flows in a southeasterly direction toward the Mississippi River.

In a few short months, I would be staying on the other end of the river, in Arkansas's Delta Country at Susan and Jeff's hunting lodge, which has easy access to the various National Wildlife Refuges in the White River watershed.

The sun was low when we started to make our way back to the marina. We were all in a mellow mood generated by hours of sun and water, and happily anticipating dry clothes and a warm evening meal. The wind was in our face and the loud hum of the boat was almost soothing. Martin skirted us past the Highway 12 bridge, just around the bend from the Prairie Creek Marina.

Wham!

I was jolted out of my reverie, and nearly out of my seat, as the boat came to a jarring halt. We looked at each other in shock. Martin had run the boat aground.

"Everyone out of the boat," Martin yelled.

We obliged, although not necessarily as quickly as he would have liked. Matt took control of determining just where the boat was grounded and how best to free it, while the rest of us stood nearby in knee-deep water. Sarah, holding Wallace, stepped back a bit further and found a rise where the water measured in inches rather than feet.

A lake policeman buzzed by at a safe distance, conveniently ignoring our frantic waves for assistance.

We were high centered, and I doubt Susan, Martin's mother, and I could have gotten the boat off that ridge. Fortunately, we had Ariel and her pole vaulter's shoulders, and Matt's six-foot-three strength. Still, it took the concerted efforts all five of us and several tries before the boat was floating again.

Once we had all climbed back aboard, including Sarah and Wallace who for obvious reasons hadn't helped with the boat rocking, Martin started off slowly. Alas, a distinct shudder told us the rudder was damaged. We stopped again and Martin made several cell phone calls before he found a friend still on the lake willing to tow us in.

"You're are going to have one hell of a moral hangover tomorrow, Martin," Sarah teased.

The sun dropped behind the cliffs to the west. I looked at the shore. Since we'd just gone past the highway bridge, the nearest land was a short distance away—swimmable even with my limited skills in the water. I was tempted to abandon ship. Sarah and Martin's house was just a short walk up the hill from there. I found out later I wasn't the only one contemplating that escape route. Instead, we all stayed put awaiting rescue.

"Look at Wallace's shirt."

Susan interrupted my evening's solace. I was enjoying a glass of red wine alone on the deck, watching the lights twinkle on the far side of the lake, contemplating sleeping in my own bed the next night. Just one ten-hour drive to go before Sauks, Andy, and I would be home.

Sarah walked out behind Susan carrying Wallace, followed by Martin and his mother. In the dim light I could see his tiny shirt said something about brother. I tried to make sense of it.

"Wallace is going to be a brother," Sarah's mother-in-law prompted.

It still wasn't sinking in. Finally, with a bit more prodding from the grandmothers it hit me.

Not only did we have Sarah standing with Wallace in the middle of Beaver Lake, we had a pregnant woman holding a toddler in the middle of the lake.

Maternal matters aren't my strong suit, so one of my first thoughts was, Damn that lake patrolman.

Epilogue

Labor Day, September 4, Rogers, Arkansas, to Sugar Land, Texas: 577 miles

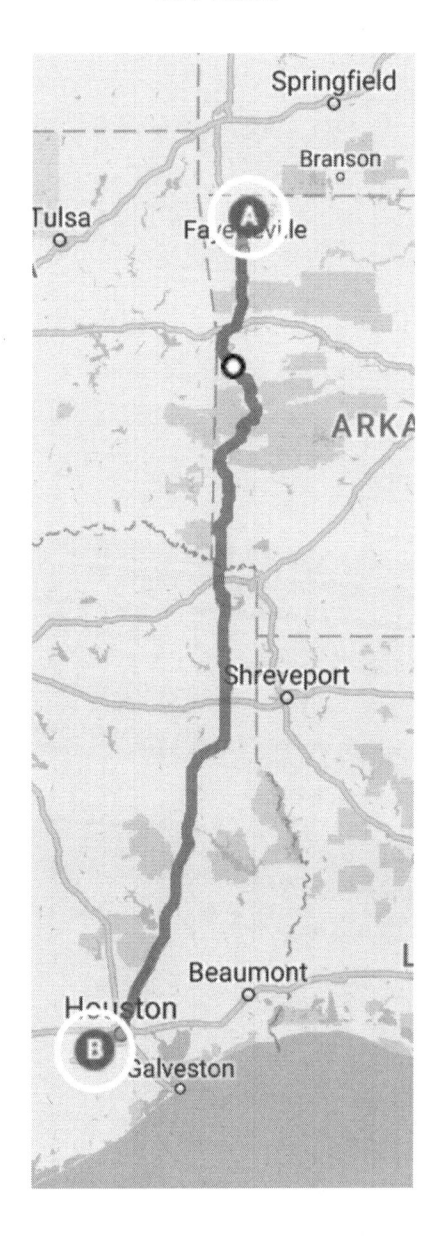

Returning to Sugar Land after an extended trip, especially one that takes me first on US 71 through the Ouachita Mountains of western Arkansas and then down US 59 through the East Texas Piney Woods, is so routine I have very little recall of the drive on Labor Day 2016 even though I'd been gone for three months.

I do remember crossing into Texas as I skirted Texarkana about five hours into the trip. After twenty-eight years, for better or worse Texas is home.

Another five hours later, I turned off the Southwest Freeway at the Grand Parkway. Both Sauks and Andy perked up. But then that may have been because I had slowed down and said something like, "Hey kids, we're home."

One thing for certain, Sauks and Andy knew our house and were glad to be back in it.

Within several months, the three of us were back on the road again. I spent much of the winter of 2016-2017 helping Susan and Jeff run their hunting lodge in Brinkley, Arkansas. So Sauks, Andy, and I made that eight-hour drive a week before Thanksgiving.

It was on that trip that the cats and I had spent the night at Susan and Jeff's nearly empty house and a strong south wind opened what I thought was a locked door the next morning. Fortunately, both Sauks and Andy quickly gave up their new-found freedom.

The three of us made the return drive to Houston for Christmas, me to catch a flight to Tampa and Sauks and Andy for a holiday week at J-Canine boarding as I had Airbnb guests.

Before New Year's, we were back on the road for lodge duty. I got a late start and was only going half way, to the historic town of Jefferson in the northeastern corner of Texas.

About fifteen miles short of my destination, I came to a grinding halt in a construction zone in Marshall.

It was after dark and a construction floodlight was glaring in my face. Since we weren't moving, Sauks and Andy decided it was more than likely their torture in the car was over. Both came out of hiding. Andy perched on my left shoulder, Sauks on my right. When traffic failed to move and I made no signs to let them out of the car, they started to scrap at each other.

Out of everything we'd experienced together on the road, perhaps none was stranger than me being caught in the midst of a cat fight conducted on my shoulders. Claws and fur were flying, both in front of my eyes and at the back of my head.

Lord only knows what the car stopped behind me thought of that mad-cap—or mad-cat if you will—show in silhouette.

The End

Postscript

I wrote the last lines of this book to the sound of Andy barfing. Determined to reach the end of this tale without interruption, I ignored him. After typing "The End," the first step in my celebration was to get up and find the hairball he'd hacked up. There is a single throw rug in the bedroom of my 2017 summer home in Tijeras, and of course that is precisely where he'd vomited. I'm sure he went out of his way to do so.

Acknowledgements

This book would not have been possible without the encouragement of numerous people. At the top of the list is Tiziana Luzzi. When I was feeling especially frustrated after losing my job in 2016, it was her suggestion to write a memoir about traveling the American West with Sauks and Andy. She also is a top-notch proofreader and fact checker.

I shared this manuscript with several other friends and family members, all of whom provided invaluable feedback. My long-time friend Susan Freeouf Becia read the entire manuscript and contributed a great deal toward the chapter "Princess Fifi," which is especially appreciated since I know it was one of the most painful days of her life. My brother Charlie Leonard also read every page. He told me to tone down the swearing a bit and was gracious about me ungratefully calling my accommodations at their lake cabin the crypt on multiple occasions. Apparently, I am the only one who has ever "complained." My niece Karin read the first chapter and told me I was on the right path when another editor begged to differ. Pamela Yenser, whom I met at a writer's conference in Albuquerque, provided feedback on my circular style of writing and let me know when she lost the thread. She also provided the excerpt from the T. S. Eliot poem.

I also want to thank all my hosts during August 2016. Reflecting on my childhood, I can only marvel at the hospitality of the relatives across the country who didn't blink an eye when my parents showed up with four kids in tow. I took that a step further when decades later I did the same with two cats. In chronological order they include: Gregory and Robbie Brinkley in Tijeras, New Mexico; Jim and Susan Becia in Littleton Colorado; John and Marcia Wild in Edwards, Colorado; my mother, Virginia Leonard in Wayne Nebraska; Charlie and Cindy Leonard, not only in Alexandria, Minnesota, but Blooming Prairie, Minnesota as well; Steve and Karin Torrey in Bloomington, Minnesota; and Martin and Sarah Brown in Rogers, Arkansas. Animals inconvenienced include Fiona, Ally, Ted, Tibby, and Ivan, although Ivan did get Fancy Feast out of the deal.

And last but not least, I owe a tremendous debt to Deane Gremmel. A personal friend and successful author, she has relentlessly pushed me forward to achieve my own dreams of writing books.

Books mentioned

Barkskins, Annie Proulx

Bridges of Madison County, Robert James Waller

Little House in the Big Woods, Laura Ingalls Wilder

The Oregon Trail: A New American Journey, Rinker Buck

The Oregon Trail, Francis Parkman

Rising from the Plains, John McPhee

The Way West, A. B. Guthrie

Under the Banner of Heaven, Jon Krakauer

Movies cited

Bridges of Madison County (1995)

Brokeback Mountain (2005)

Butch Cassidy and the Sundance Kid (1969)

Dances with Wolves (1990)

Fargo (1996)

Hell or High Water (2016)

Nebraska (2013)

One Nation under Dog (2012)

Pulp Fiction (1994)

Terms of Endearment (1983)

The Long Riders (1980)

The Texas Chainsaw Massacre (1974)

The Wizard of Oz (1939)

Printed in Great Britain
by Amazon